BROKEN

L.Loera

authorHOUSE®

AuthorHouse™
1663 Liberty Drive
Bloomington, IN 47403
www.authorhouse.com
Phone: 1-800-839-8640

First published by AuthorHouse 8/4/2011

ISBN: 978-1-4520-2535-3 (sc)
ISBN: 978-1-4520-2536-0 (e)

Library of Congress Control Number: 2011910012

Printed in the United States of America

Cover illustrated by Luis F. Villareal Jr

The reason for my story is to reach victims all over the world in hope of inspiring you to come forward and bring to justice more sex offenders as I did. That first step is the most crucial in any kind of recovery and is extremely difficult. We all know that any kind of abuse is very traumatic for every victim, and what I have found, is that every victim's reaction is completely different yet not all accepted by society as they claim. Victims are not always women as most people think. Violators, rapists and sexual offenders are given many chances to re-do their lives and pick up where they left off when they get out of jail if they ever spend a day in jail. But us victims, forever live in a dark gloomy world, full of suspicious people and find it very hard to continue with our normal lives ever again. We live a life sentence of depression, guilt, shame and fear because of our attackers, and that is not the way it should be. Our system should be able to understand, guild and help us to a life time of therapy paid for by our government and/or the offender for changing our entire life as well as our loved once. We are left with distorted minds for the way they treated us. Our system should realize that just as every "case" is different, so is our response to our traumatic experience and to the therapy received, if any. Unfortunately, some victims turn to drugs, alcohol, lose or gain weight, depression or even suicide, leaving children, families and friends behind. Others turn to prostitution or just having multiple sexual partners'. Others turn to same sex partners for fear of the opposite sexual partner hurting them too. And others give up having a social, sexual, or spiritual life all together. Some victims live hating men for the rest of their lives, blaming the rest of the world for their anger and when they totally loose control and snap, they forget why they had so much anger built up inside. Many victims have hurt, tortured and killed men in acts of passion, anger and/or revenge. And the punishment these victims receive, is much harsher than the one there attackers received for distorting their lives! We inmates are rarely treated with respect or dignity yet expected to forgive and defiantly forget what was done to us.

The Police officer's were on the prowl for a drunken woman to come out of the bar to take advantage of her. I ended up being that woman, only I wasn't drunk, but they still found a way to violate me. They took advantage of their badges, their guns, their authority and worse of all, me! What puzzled them was how I had concealed enough evidence and or witnesses to bring them to justice?

I want to dedicate this book to my only daughter
Adriana whom I've loved too much
She's the only one that's been there for me and with me
When no one else was. Thank you baby

This book is for you.

The ones whom invaded in Body,

My Mind, my Spirit and My Entire World.

My name is not important, but the reason for this story is.

I'm sure that some women out there can relate to what I am about to share on.

I was humiliated and laughed at by a couple of buddies that decided they would violate me on a dark lonely road.

"I didn't do anything sexually to her! I was just following orders!" One of them claimed!

The other one, had an extremely difficult time remembering which one of all the girls he had done this to, I was.

Chapter 1

I use to be a happy go lucky girl, even at the age of thirty-five. This was my age at time of this "incident" as they addressed it. I always thought of myself as a girl, not a woman. Always felt so young, pretty and so full of life. I had a lot of spunk, and my energy level was endless. I overcame any obstacles that came my way; in fact it was quite interesting to conquer new challenges in my daily life. I felt so proud of myself for not having to rely on anybody for to help raise my daughter. I was on top of the world along with my little girl, been a great provider for her, just as I had promised the day I left her father. Being a single mother was so much fun to me I couldn't imagine why some women complained about the children.

Though my daughter was still too little to remember when we left her dad. I made sure to give her plenty of love for both of us. Worked as much overtime as I possible could to give her what she needed, wanted and more. I felt so confident and tough enough to handle any situation that came my way. Why not, I thought, after all, I had fought with both boys and girls before, in school while trying to fit in. So of course I could handle myself from any jerk that might want to hurt me. I had lots of friends not enemies. Not giving it much thought, I knew I was loved by the people I considered my friends.

Everyone I knew, that were over the age of twenty-five were too serious and so angry. Too grumpy, tired and constantly complaining about bills, their spouse, the car, not enough money but mostly, the children. So I knew I was lucky to have what I thought was a blessed life, again. I enjoyed my daughter so much, taking her to kids birthday party's, eat at fancy restaurants (which we both love), movies, carnivals, the park, swimming, the library and everywhere she wanted to go. So I refused to live my life as though it was going to be over soon. Besides, I deserved to have a little fun too and treated myself to partying, since I worked so hard to support us both. I even worked when I was married so I didn't know how to depend on anyone but me. I had always been the life of the party and my favorite thing to do was to make new friends where ever I was at, with friends, at family gatherings and/or the local bar or clubs.

It wasn't always a walk in the park but it was fun and I always came through. At times I even came to believe that my sisters were a little jealous of me since they were all married and were tied down to a husband and had more children than I. And I was a single mother with only one gorgeous well-behaved daughter, and loving it.

Against my family's advice, I'd still go out on weekends and unfortunately, this behavior eventually turned into my using and abusing drugs at one point. But through all this, I managed to still care for my daughter and attend all of her daycare and school functions.

To understand my story I would have to tell you a little bit about my Family, Friends and my Past.

Chapter 2

My parents met, dated and married in Juarez Mexico in the mid 1960's. They immediately moved to New Mexico where my father had been employed for a few years before their wedding. My mother tells her sad story of how she missed her mom, dad and siblings and her entire world as she now felt so alone in that house by herself all day long. My Father worked six days a week, twelve hour shifts on a Diary farm. The owners had small apartments for his employees and their families to live in around the ranch. But my mother felt isolated, lonely and very bored with nothing to see but cows and hay for miles to her surroundings. She loved my father so much that she never complained to him. But my father knew that there was more to life than this and wanted to spend more time with her and be happy. They both felt they were missing out on something and wanted to go find it.

So they made the decision to move to Chicago Ill where his family lived and there were more than enough jobs up north. My father began working a few days after they arrived and my mother befriended a great neighbor whom was also a newly wed, and they became real good friends. They had a very unique and interesting kind of friendship, my mother struggled to learn the English language and her new friend did not know Spanish at all. So they made a pact to teach each other the other's language and a beautiful sisterhood was born between them. A few years into there marriage, my mother was finally pregnant with my oldest sister and felt so blessed, they just kept having more. Even though they had five little girls, I think my mother kind of hoped for a boy too. But my father loved God so much, that he strongly believed he had a plan for everyone and was always very proud of us all. My mom's friend had as many children as she did and were inseparable as well.

As we grew up and started school, my father enrolled us all in one of the best Catholic School in Chicago, he thought It'd best for the entire family, since he wanted the best for us and we were very involved in our catholic community. Like most Hispanic families, my parents' hopes and dreams of giving their children the best education and upbringing was of high priority. My mom was a homemaker and took her role very seriously; she cooked, cleaned and was a great role model. She cooked at our Church's Convent for the entire parish of Nuns and Priests. She managed to volunteer on a regular basis, and still take us to the park after dinner.

At school, the Nuns taught us good manners, discipline and to love and respect one another. I tagged along with my mom to the convent, while she prepared their supper and attended the many different activities with the nuns that were being held that day. The Rosary, Prayers, Bible studies or just have conversations with the Nuns. I enjoyed their stories and the way they all got along. It was a remarkable sisterhood, I never saw them arguing or disagreeing with each other. They would also do their sewing and ironing and cleaning like everyone else. But they smiled as they did their choirs and swept the floors. It made you want to join their way of living. They had a permanent smile on their face as they sang Christian hymns and worship songs and I loved the feel of peace and love that was felt in the convent. I always wanted to be around them, be like them and feel like they did. I liked to think that this was the way it was going to be like in Haven.

Every time we had a school play I was the first to sign up as well as participate in all of the church extra curriculum activities. In fact most of us girls wanted to become nuns when I grew up. But I knew my feelings were particularly different because I loved God and the world so much that I was sure that that was going to be my vocation.

My dad also volunteered to do the maintenance and the landscaping for the church. It wasn't a chore or a burden to him, it was a passion he had for helping others with his unconditional love and maybe that's why I was so close to him. This was the kind of person he was and I wanted to grow up to be just like him. I wondered how you ever get over a person like my dad. I loved my school, the staff and the church most of them were nuns and priests back then. No one would ever dare to harm each other. These were devoted religious people whom were strict but treated us with dignity and respect, because everyone followed the rules and regulations, and so did I.

We respected and feared God so much that we just didn't want for the school to have to discipline us for breaking any rules. We wanted to please God, our parents and the school we were all so proud of.

Chapter 3

The day came in which they hired regular civilians as teachers, janitors and cooks. We all got along and had no reason to fear anyone. One day we were introduced to our new homeroom teacher, she I remember was tall, slim and had a noticeably fake smile, but she seamed like a nice person at first. We were innocent children at that time and didn't pay much attention to details or peoples cruel intentions. So we saw her as a new teacher that the Lord had blessed our school with. My younger sister and I were classmates, but were in different grades. That year I suppose they were remodeling the dinning room or something because we had lunch in our classroom, during which the teacher noticed my sister and I traded our desert with each other which was fruit. At this she became very angry, very quickly.

She then stood in front of me and with a strict and harsh voice ordered me to eat my apple. My sister then explained to her that I didn't like apples so my mother would buy me oranges instead. This explanation raised the teacher's temper and she turned to me with a frown then smiled and told me to go into the classroom's closet and stay their till I ate all of it. At the age of about eight years old that I was, just like many children, I was afraid of the dark, but she walked me towards it anyway. I began to cry frantically as she closed the door behind me, in that dark and crowded closet. Just then, my sister also began to cry as loud as I was. I suppose she felt my anguish, since we were so close and had been brought up to be companionate with each other. So the teacher placed her in there with me and gave us more apples that she had taken from other children, she told us to eat the seeds as well as the stems.

All but one of the other children in the class were quit and didn't move an inch, fearing they too could do something that would make her turn on them as well. Ana, she was the only one whom seamed to find the teacher's behavior amusing, she laughed as if some one had just said a hilarious joke. She became the teacher's pet almost instantly for being her only fan.

Minutes later as we were talking amongst us and threw the last of the stem in back of a tall cabinet at the end of the closet, to our misfortune, Ana opened the door and witnessed what we had done. We begged her not to tell, but she happily and loudly announced it so the entire class would laugh at our next punishment for what we had done.

To our surprise, no one was laughing but her, by the time the teacher stood at the door we were shaking as we held each other and cried uncontrollably again. We were afraid of what more she would do to us next, but nothing prepared us for what she made us do. She moved the cabinet and scooped up the stems and seeds from the floor full of hair, dirt and dead insects, then put them in the palm of our hands and made us eat them in front of the entire class. Everyone was quit and disguised at what she made us do. Some of them even had tears in their eyes but wiped them away before the teacher saw them and pick on them too.

At the end of the day, while making our way towards the stairs to the cold and snowy outdoors. Ana stood at the top of the stairs laughing at us for the filth we had eaten. We kept walking passed her until she insulted my sister for being overweight. With that, I lost total control of myself and launched at her with all my strength and hit her as hard as I could and couldn't stop throwing blows at her until the nuns managed to peel me off of her.

She didn't even know how to fight as I recall. She cried like a baby and tried to run and escape the fury I had build up, and so I got a tight grip on her and was releasing all the anger, humiliation and frustration I felt towards her and the teacher I suppose.

After coming home with a suspension note for the first time in my life, my parents couldn't imagine what I had done to deserve this. I couldn't break there hearts by telling them the truth, but my sister didn't feel it was right for me to have to be punished for what she though I had a right to do. So, without hesitating, she told them everything we had both gone through that day. To my surprise, they hugged us and cried almost as much as we did. So the next morning, they both took us to school and went straight to Principal Father Charles Office. Even though my mom wanted to go to our classroom and force the stupid teacher to eat the filth she had forced us to eat the day before. My dad held her back and promised to handle this matter, the right way.

We were in the office for a good hour until we told Father Charles and sister Lupita what we were put through in front of the entire class. She took a few minutes to regain herself after shedding a few tears, and blaming herself for hiring her. The Principal and the Assistant Principal both must have taken the right measures since, I don't remember seen that teacher after that. Our classmates also told Sister Lupita they too feared this teacher and she vowed to never allow her or anyone else to harm us that way again, and no one ever did. This is the only horror story that ever happened at our school. Our school and our home were full of valuable educational values and great Christian morals. We were family.

Chapter 4

The entire alumni singed up for and enjoyed all of the many school plays, choir and sports and recreational activities. Teachers, parents, staff members and children always had a magnificent time. We had many clubs like Drama, Spelling Bee and Science fair, Carnivals and School Dances.

Life in Chicago was beautiful and safe, serious but fun. We lived a very structured, simple though busy life, I remember. The sweet aroma of my mother's hot breakfast would be our wake up call every single morning. We happily jumped out of bed and rushed to get ready to be the first to enjoy my mom's wonderful breakfast. We thanked her in anticipation for the delicious meals she'd prepare us every single time. She was the best cook in the entire world. Off to school with a big smile on our face right after a hearty breakfast. After school I'd meet my mother at our parish's kitchen as she would finish cooking for them then off to go have our supper, do our homework, than fun at the park.

We'd shower then get ready for the next school day. We enjoyed our lives every day and night back then. We lead a disciplined and routine life that we absolutely loved. This was our lifestyle ever since I can remember. The only time my mother would ever be upset with my dad was on Friday nights. See, my father liked to drink upon arriving home from work, just about every other Friday night.

My mother never drank alcohol she didn't like it so she never got accustomed to his drinking, even though it was only once or twice a month. It didn't matter to her how often a person drank, "it just wasn't fit" she said, there was no reason for drinking. He never bothered anyone not even her, he just sat there watching TV and watch us all make fools of ourselves, we all took turns showing him silly tricks like jumping rope, playing dolls, or talking about a school. We all laughed and played as my mother finished up the nights work in the kitchen.

Every Saturday morning, we woke up early and give my mom a break from her daily chores, and so it was the kid's day to clean the house and make breakfast so she would sleep late. Of course she never did sleep late. After breakfast we went grocery shopping and raided stores for shoes, clothes and toys of course. Then we'd go home and enjoy the rest of the day with just the family, "Us". On Sundays just before Church Service we attended Sunday school then joined our parents for mass.

After Church service we would head out to the beautiful Lake Michigan which was our favorite place to go to. Our family, friends and/or neighbor were already their, anxiously for us to arrive. The men did all the cooking so to be nice and give their wives a break I guess. And then we'd get in the water, eat and play with or against the parents, and had all kinds of family fun. When we didn't go to the lake, we'd still have fun visiting relatives or friends, or go to the movies, roller-skating, the baseball games or the many museums Chicago is so famous for. We had so many friends and relatives in Chicago and its surroundings that I thought we knew absolutely everyone in the state. In the winter we'd go ice skating, or go to the many different parks or walk threw beautiful downtown to catch up on our window-shopping and enjoy the beautiful city.

Every winter they place a huge, gigantic Christmas tree downtown and people ice skate all around it and we loved to just take all that beauty in. I am proud to say I loved my childhood and am grateful for both my parent's tender loving care. I thought of my family, as been one of the most perfect and blessed families in the world. My parents had endless ideas of fun every day of the year in the most wonderful city in the world we lived in.

They always made sure they provided us with all they had and more. A well balanced lifestyle was a necessity for a healthy mind, body and spirit was our motto. Mental health was as important as our physical health is what they believed. So we played as hard as we worked and we pulled together as a family. The word impossible was not in our vocabulary. Our stability in our Christian life was solid as a rock. Or so we thought. Every year in the summer, we'd vacation in Mexico but what we enjoyed the most was taking that road trip down there. We all looked forward to spending time with our extended family and friends. My father owned several properties in Mexico and he'd remodeled the homes that needed it. Then he'd buy another piece of land and build a house their then sell it before went back to home. The weekend before we left, my father would throw a huge block party. We had a cook out and enjoying the pool we had in his favorite piece of land. He said that one was our land so he was never going to sell it or get rid of it, so this is the one we came to every year.

Chapter 5

Then one day, on Sept 3rd 1980 to be exact, we were on our way back from visiting family in Rochelle Illinois, that's about an hour away from Chicago. My father complained of a small lump on the side of his neck and said it had been hurting him all day, so my mom told him they would make an appointment with his Doctor the following day and they did. To everyone's horror, the Doctor called late that cold evening as we were preparing for bed. Since my father thought he didn't understand clearly, he asked me to pick up the other telephone and translate for him, so I did, but nothing prepared me for what I heard. The Doctor said that after he had preformed several exams, they had concluded my father had Leukemia!

Leukemia, the most horrible word in Medical History, I knew. He needed to be admitted into the Hospital first thing the next morning. That only meant one thing, which was that he was going to die! And nobody could save him, not the Doctor, not the Nuns nor the Priests nor Us. We all just stood there staring at one another, speechless and clueless to what our next move was suppose to be. My dad had always been the one to guide our agenda, but he must have been scared too that night as he hung up the phone and just walked into their bedroom and closed the door.

We each returned to our rooms and crawled into bed as we prayed as hard as we cried ourselves to sleep that night. Our lives became numb after only having him for a short time after that day. The Doctors had guessed he would only live five to ten years but not more than that. It was all too sudden. It seemed like a bad dream we would wake up from and he would be fine. Deep down inside me I was waiting for the Doctor to call us back and say he was sorry he had made a mistake, and we could bring my daddy home again. But the Doctor never called back, he never apologized and it wasn't fair. My Father was in and out of the hospital for the next month and unfortunately, children weren't allowed to have long visits so we only saw him very little then.

My world came to a completely halt as my father passed away about six weeks later, on October 20th 1980. Even the Doctors were shocked whom were certain he'd live longer. Several of my parent's life long friends were at the hospital visiting my father that evening. He had received his first Chemotherapy treatment just that morning. At about seven that evening his friends had just said their good byes and were walking down the hall towards the elevator. My father began to feel extremely sick not being able to breath. He was gasping for air and told my mother to go get help. My mother ran out to the hall way screaming frantically for the doctor. But when they came into his room and tried so hard to resuscitate him back to life, there was nothing they could do. There was nothing anybody could do, not even God could bring him back. My Father passed away at seven O' Clock that awful cold winter night.

My aunt and uncle stayed with us children while my mother was at my father's side in the hospital that night. I still remember that awful night as if it were just yesterday.

My mother entered the front door and stood in the foyer for a long while, just staring at us all. Her eyes were red and swollen from crying so much and she looked like she had just aged about forty years. She tried to gather the right words to tell us that our father had just passed away. But there were no right words to tell us that my dad was never coming back.

She broke down and cried so much and so loud, it scared me even more since we had never seen her cry that way before. We instantly knew that our worst fear had just occurred. But she couldn't contain herself no more, we saw it in her eyes, she told us what had happened without saying a word. She cried and shook her head and grabbed her hair as she felt the pain inside of her and wanted to run in desperation. She was incoherent and angry and frightened all at once. She refused to accept the fact that my father was now dead. All this time we had been sitting in the living room, waiting quietly and patiently and on our best behavior. Waiting her arrival and praying my father would return along with her. But all that didn't matter anymore. All that was now gone, all those weeks of praying and believing he would make a huge recovery and going to prove them wrong. He had to live he had to live for us, for me. If I could just go see him and tell him that I loved him, tell him not to die. Tell him that I want him back tell him that I thank him for being who he was, than maybe he would open his eyes again. I wanted to see him smile at me just one more time.

We ran into her arms and held on to her and we cried for what seemed like hours, we grieved and it hurt. I ran to the restroom and kicked the door as hard as I could. I couldn't believe her I wanted to go and see him open his eyes for me. I knew that if he heard my voice he's come back to me. He knew I loved him so, he knew I couldn't live without him, he knew he couldn't die. He needed to hear my voice and my sister's voice to remember that he couldn't leave us yet. Why did he die? I thought. How could he leave me? But he had died, and was never coming back.

I was thirteen years old when he passed away and the thought of not having him with me or seen him no more was unbearable to me. I walked but had no sense of direction, I ate but the food seamed to have lost all taste in it. I looked but saw straight pass everything. I hated the birds for chirping and singing. I wanted to go yell at the neighbor's for there music seemed to be too loud, and I just didn't see any point in life without him any more. Life kept going though, the stores were still open and the phone kept on ringing. I kept waking up every morning and my daddy wasn't there anymore. I didn't understand why or how God had permitted such tragedy? No one seemed to notice that we were now incomplete, there was some one missing, the most important person in the world to me, yet they didn't care. Everything seemed to be so vague now.

He was a very hard working Father who had more love than anyone can ever imagine, why would God want to take him away. I didn't understand. I thought we were an enormously blessed family, he didn't deserve this and neither did we. All we were left with, as we grieved for my daddy, were pictures to remember him by and the endless memories we will never let go of. And an aching pain in our heart that only a little girl whom lost her father could only understand. People were hugging us tight and certainly speaking in some sort of foreign language seemed like, but the sound resembled that of someone speaking inside of a pail, with an echo that was endless. But nothing they said made any sense.

He was loved by everyone who knew him. For years we grieved for the most wonderful father, husband and friend that ever lived, this would be the most painful feeling I had experienced, up until then. Michael Brady wasn't even half the man my father was. He never let anybody down and would be the first to help where ever help was needed. My dad was a great Hero, to us, and the heart and soul of our family. Well that is pretty much how I've always thought of him, and always will...

To this day I cry like a baby as I still mourn his death like if it was just yesterday.

He was my father, my protector and my friend.

Chapter 6

We all flew together on the same airplane from Chicago Illinois to El Paso Texas, then drove to Cd. Juarez, Mexico, to lay him to rest near his mother's home. It felt wrong to go to the same place we vacationed to every year since we were born, to go back to where we had so many fantastic memories. As my father's lifeless body was in a different car, I realized that this would be our last trip together, as a family. To this day I don't know why my mother agreed to lay him to rest near his mother instead of near us. We resented her for this. He would be left behind, in a different city, in a different state not too mention in a different country. We wanted him near us.

We weren't ready to let go yet, we didn't know how too, we were never taught to say good bye for ever. But we were too young to argue or disagree with my mother. We wouldn't dare contradict our parent's decisions. We would never question their authority and or the decisions adults made. We were very obedient kids regardless of the situation. Besides we were still in shock too and took a long time to snap out of it. Everything changed for us when we came back home without my father. We were in for a rude awakening and it was going to get ugly.

As if my father's passing wasn't traumatic enough, that Christmas was the worst one we ever spent. My mother sent my oldest sister and me to buy my youngest sisters a Santa Clause gift. As her words were still confusingly gathering in my mind. I asked her "what Santa Clause gifts?" When she explained to me that the gifts we bought were going to be from Santa. I felt so disappointed and foolish for being that naïve, I was thirteen years old and still believed in Santa. My mother hadn't realized that they had cocooned us from so many things in life. I don't know how I went on without knowing such an important fact of life. I felt so stupid and ignorant and wondered what else I was oblivious to.

The day before that dreadful Christmas, my youngest sisters Godparents came to drop off their gifts. As they handed them their gifts, my baby sister said to them "You forgot my other sister's gifts, where are they"? Of Corse my mother felt embarrassed and tried to hush her but she just kept insisting on wanting to know if they were going to bring us something and when, "hurry tomorrow is Christmas so you don't have much time" she said. They left with the promise of bringing us our gifts the following day. But they never returned.

My mother couldn't afford to keep us in private school any longer. This religious and educational way of life we were bought up in was now a considered a luxury. We felt betrayed from this spiritual structural life we loved so much. We considered our church and school family but we were unaware that it cost money and was very expensive and my father paid for us to receive this kind of education. And we did not have the means to continue any more. We finished off the school year then we switched to public school and we were not accustomed to that different kind of lifestyle at all.

It was difficult to adjust to a classroom full of three to four times more students and they refused to listen to the teachers. Kids would constantly interrupt each other and the teacher. The dining area was now a cafeteria room with students sitting on the tables instead of the chairs. No one said grace before any meal at all. In fact, they ridiculed who ever attempted to talk about God. It was not only a different school to us, but it was like a totally different kind of world, a different universe. There was no discipline or manners much less respect for others. They were as different as night and day to us. We were so ignorant and totally unaware of this much difference in people. No one seemed to care who we were or what we had just gone through.

We simply now had to hide what we were so proud of and how we were raised in order to not stand out more than we already did. We had already been through a lot and being cast outs was not in our agenda. We had to down size to a much smaller living space. My older sister's Godparents offered us their basement one bedroom apartment, and my mother accepted, in need of some kind of support I suppose. She must have figured they would comfort her and were going to be there for her as they promised her at my daddy's funeral. They did visit my mother on a regular basis the first few weeks, but they slowly backed away. We all had to make due with what we had now which was not much at all.

No more having the comfort of each one of us having our own huge bedroom. No more spacious living room, open kitchen and dinning room, large foyer and no more roomy basement and attic to play in. No more going to the park after dinner for some quality family fun and exercise. No more playing outside with our childhood friends after doing our homework with friends. No more preparing our school uniforms for the next day. And definitely, No more daddy to jump on and play with while he attempted to walked in the house when he was home from work. We now had to take public transportation to get to school.

Chapter 7

We walked two blocks to the bus stop and then catch two different buses to and from school every day now. The cold, dark winter months were the worst for us because we had to walk threw snow, muddy slush, ice and sleet. We'd walk alone for what seemed like endless blocks and taking long bus rides. One day we missed the bus in the morning and we sure learned fast never to do that again. We walked about six miles to school that day and were wet and half frozen by the time we arrived to school. From that day on, we made sure to never miss the bus again. This situation was a constant reminder that my daddy was not with us any longer. Our family car broke down and my mother sold it not knowing what was wrong with it. We were living in a nightmare and never going back to the happy life we longed for still.

The rain added to the freezing temperature that made our tears nearly freeze running down our face. It was impossible for us to not miss the way our life was when we were a complete family, but we never complaint to my mother. We didn't want to hurt her anymore than she already was. We lived in the front end part of the basement due to the fact that the back end was used as a storage space. The Land Lords lived upstairs in the first floor of the house and both of there sons shared the attic. They also had a spacious back yard which we were no longer welcomed to since we were now tenants not friends.

My mother realized they too, slowly began to stop visiting and or listening to her cries of how she missed my dad. Luckily we only lived there for about two years. These people had first met my dad in his teenage years before he married my mother. My mom had come to love this couple and respected them like parents, since they were twice her age. So they decided these were the perfect people to baptize there first born daughter, my oldest sister.

Money was tight then, so my younger sister, my mother and I began knitting complete baby outfits with blankets to help our financial situation. I have to admit it was kind of fun to me because I had always been a creative person and enjoyed spending time with my family. We worked together as a family and that was enough for me. We sold the outfits and that was an enormous financial blessing for us. One day while we were in school, my Mother and baby sister were home alone. The landlord took it upon himself to unlock the rear door and just walked in, directly towards her and attempted to force himself on her. My poor mother was terrified and couldn't believe he had done that. She then slapped him and pushed him back out the door.

Since she began to raise her voice, he must have decided he didn't want his family to find out what he had done and walked away the same way he came in. My mother then moved a heavy dresser against the door in order to keep him out as her heart pounded uncontrollably with fear. How could this man, whom my father loved so much and looked up to, try to take advantage of a still grieving widow she though. After crying so much for a few weeks, my mom got a hold on herself and faced the facts.

This was one of my dad's most trusted friends, so she knew she couldn't break his wives heart by telling her what he had tried to do to her. This woman and her daughter had been two of the few people who visited my mother every day for a few months after my father passed. My mother just lay their crying, grieving not having the strength to care for herself or my baby sister. These women helped her until she was able to get up in the morning and care for the baby at least.

She couldn't possibly hurt them by telling them what he had tried to do to her. She thought about what her next move should be, and I could only imagine how terribly frightened she must have been as she cried herself to sleep at night. She didn't think it'd be wise to stay there any longer, for fear of him coming after one of us too. So as we all left for school the next morning, she came to the conclusion of moving near her only sister in Texas. Besides, she had plenty of family whom offered there help and support out there. After all, she was awful lonely and even more scared than ever now.

And for the first time since she married, she was without a partner to protect her. My oldest sister now had a boyfriend who she wanted to live with. My younger sister refused to go to school. And I just couldn't adjust at my new school either, and my youngest sisters needed my mother's undivided attention. So my mother knew she needed guidance and help with her daughters. We had many family and friends in Chicago, yet my mother felt that no one here was competent enough to assist her in her new role as a single mother. We were considered one of the most enjoyable families in Chicago amongst everyone we knew. But for some reason, we didn't seem to be welcomed anymore or fit in. My Mother made several attempts for us to visit family or friends like we use to when my father was alive, but we had seemed to become a burden to everyone. We started seen the change in people's behavior towards us.

They were quite and distant, telling us they were on there way out and basically making excuses for us to leave. So we just stopped visiting and gave up all sorts of entertainment all together. My mother's now single parental task had became an impossible mission to carry out by herself. I realize the importance of my little sisters three and eight years old, needed my mother's hugs, love and affection at the time. But it was almost impossible for her to be able to function as a mom when she herself had lost her husband and soul mate.

We were in so much need of our mother but she was severely depressed and unable to cope with reality. Certainly she was in great need of help, guidance and affection as much as we were. But she was unable of asking for help, she felt the world had forsaken her and God had abandoned her. That's when I became angrier with God and the angels and heaven and didn't care to hear anything the Nuns and the Priests were praying and saying to us anymore. I didn't care about anything except wanting my father back. All I knew was that God had taken away the most important person in my entire life, and no one could ever bring him back, not even him. I didn't know why this was happening to us? I wanted to know why he had taken my father away from us.

We were moving to another city and yet another Public School without a car and my mother was a total train wreck. She didn't know how to manage anything at all, we were convinced that without my father, we couldn't survive out their. My father was the provider, the bread winner and paid all the bills and drove us every where. My mother had been a homemaker, house wife and mother since they married. She didn't know how to run the entire family on her own. Besides who was going to love us forever like he had promise us?

Chapter 8

We had only been in town for three day at my Aunt's home in Juarez. My mother turned to her only sister for a shoulder to cry on. Ironically my aunt was my mother's sister and her husband was one of my father's brothers but was nothing like my father. In fact that night, she told us we were too many to handle and we had to leave their house as soon as possible. I'll never forget the day she kicked us out of her house. We stayed out of there house and out of their way all day, but I guess it wasn't enough. On what would have been our third night stay, we returned kind of lat since we had been house hunting all day, and they were having dinner.

We said hello and walked right passed them towards the back yard, tired and hungry from walking all day long. We walked behind my mother like a hen and her chicks walking towards a pond. To our unexpected surprise, my uncle startled us as he slammed his fist on the kitchen table and very angrily pushed his plate away. He yelled at us Damning us to hell for interrupting his dinner and intruding in there lives. At that my mom started crying softly in the yard as did we, not knowing what to do or where to go. We could hear them arguing out loud but couldn't make out what they were saying. After my aunt calmed him down a little bit and finished their dinner, my aunt came outside and told us we couldn't stay there any longer.

So the first few days we lived with other family members in Juarez Mexico, and my oldest sister and her boyfriend moved away. My father owned a few houses in Juarez at the time of his death yet no one ever paid my mom the remaining balance they owed him. They all told my mom that because we were all Americans, and my father didn't leave a will or a Power of Attorney letter. We weren't entitled to a single penny from anyone. She didn't know any better since my dad was the one who always handled their real estate businesses and financial situations.

She was still in mourning and wasn't thinking straight I suppose. She honestly thought she couldn't do anything about it since they all said the same thing to her. She believed them and didn't even think to seek legal advice or do the research for our sake. So they kept their houses without ever paying them in full, lucky break for them I guess.

My father had begun to build a house in the center of the land he held aside for us but was incomplete. So we moved in their, until we could find a place in El Paso. The unfinished house had four walls, no roof, no floor, no windows, no doors but it had a huge rock wall around it. And for the first time since our Father had died, we tried to find some kind of positive humor in the situation we were in. So we thought of this as a huge cement box we can call home, and at least we had our privacy. Also, we no indoor plumbing, but an out door bathroom with a toilet and that was good enough for us at the time.

Thank God the next door neighbor allowed us to use the electricity and water from his meter which was very generous of him. So he ran an electrical cord and a water hose over the wall for us to use. He was the only man whom had paid off his home in full to my father before he died. So we were very grateful to him and never abused his generosity or the electricity and water since this was the only way we could show our appreciation to him. My mothers aunt and her kids came to help us out as soon as they found out we were their. They were the only ones that were so kind to us. They treated us with respect and dignity and actually felt sorry we would never return to that world we were accustomed to. It's as if they were the only once that really understood us. I remember they gave us an allowance on Sunday which was extremely admirable since they were our age. We became real good friends with those cousins as they guided us as best they could. We did not have a vehicle so we had to walk every where we needed to go. We had to learn the art of clipping coupons and keep up with the store specials within our new neighborhood area stores. Some streets in Juarez were not even paved back then, so it made it that much harder for us since we weren't use to that. Public transportation was not at all fascinating either, for it was full of people smelled of sweat, food and urine. But we tried to make the most of it anyway. We searched tirelessly for an apartment and couldn't wait to move. We craved a real home with indoor plumbing again. We craved anything that resembled a decent home without worrying about it raining on us since we still didn't have a roof.

Unfortunately, there were more fiends waiting to attach! The lady, who lived behind our property, took advantage of my poor mother as well, just as many other people did. She conned my mother into selling her that land we had left, reminding her she too could take it away from us for free if she wanted to. She reminded her that we Americans had no rights in Mexico when it came to inheritance or property. So of coarse my mother, believed her since she still hadn't educated herself on the Mexican property laws and regulations. So she sold her the property without discussing it with anyone at all, not even us. Unfortunately she only paid her less than one percent of the lands value. My father's oldest brother also conned her into selling him another land my father had in San Elizario Texas, for less than one percent of its value.

He also charged her those one thousand dollars. He claimed to have paid to cross my fathers' body and casket across the border. We found out years later that this was a lie because the funeral home from Chicago had already included that in there price. But my mother still paid him that money because she believed him. I'll never understand how so many people, including our own flesh and blood took advantage of a grieving widow in so many ways. Hard to believe they posses a heart or have a conscience since they only thought of their own personal gain. My father was good to all these people and shared all he had with them, yet they treated us all like vagabonds. Oddly enough, that's exactly how I felt.

Chapter 9

Life here was so different now from when we use to vacation every year. We didn't have all the commodities we were used too every summer. My father would arrange a comfortable place for us to stay while he bought a new property, built a house and sold it in just the few weeks we were their. He made this particular acre of land, suitable enough for us to play, run and swim in the pool we built in the back for us. He kept this land for us, he said this was ours and he would never sell it. Now the pool was cracked and full of green fungus we would not dare come close to. We longed for that life in which we were so happy and use to in Chicago ever since we were born. None of us went to church any more, not even my mother.

Christmas was especially hard for us, not only for the great gifts and goodies we shared. But because Christmas had a more sentimental religious value for us as we celebrated Jesus' birth more than our presents. We cried so much for having to live in a life full of disappointments and having to grow up so suddenly. We blame God for taking my father away. Unfortunately we were only able to afford gifts for my two youngest sisters since we had very limited resources. My younger sister and I rebelled for a while hanging out with the wrong crowd and refusing to go to school. But it didn't last long since we still had a conscience and good education, we didn't want to hurt my mother. My oldest sister and her boyfriend had finally come back and we were thrilled they were going to live with us. They were also expecting a baby now, and that added yet another challenge to our confusing situation.

My mom always said she'd kick us out of the house if we got pregnant, since having a baby out of wedlock was totally unacceptable. Oh my God! We thought my mom was going to tell her to leave and never come back. But to our surprise she didn't kick them out and we were relieved to know she accepted them both. We were a bit upset she had gotten away with breaking the rules though. But we were learning to move on now no matter what life threw our way.

Chapter 10

Almost three months had past when we finally moved to El Paso. Even thought the place we moved into was once again a one bedroom tiny apartment. Unfortunately we were now getting accustomed to live in such circumstances. This was all my mother could afford, and was better than having an outdoor bathroom. We struggled to fit in at school once more, but it was virtually impossible for us to get used to the coax. My mother did the best she could to raise us and had a difficult time managing her little bit of money. Making it all last for bills, food and the necessities, and so there was very little or none left for clothes much less for entertainment.

But she managed to provide a roof over our head and that was more than enough for us all. The day my sister gave birth to her beautiful baby girl, my mother had a rude awakening that changed all of our lives. My mom passed out during my sisters eighteen hour labor experience since she had a difficult time giving birth. I suppose my mom finally understood that she had to go out and find herself a job to support us all. Including her brand new granddaughter, since my sister was still a teenager and still in high school. She knew that my sister and her boyfriend weren't going to be able to support the baby by themselves and needed her help.

My mother landed a custodial job at the University of Texas At El Paso. Working was which an inconvenience to her at first since she wasn't use to having a real job. My father always worked and she stayed home for years. At first she walked around like a zombie, not talking to anyone, cleaning and taking out the trash. Crying on her lunch break instead of eating became her daily routine. By the time my poor mother arrived at home, she was dead tired and dragged her feet in the house sat on the couch crying for at least an hour. She'd angrily scold and curse my dad for have left her alone in this world. She was angry at him as if it was his fault he had this deadly cancer that claimed his life. She was angry she now had to carry this extremely heavy load all by herself. I can't imagine how difficult it was for her and didn't blame her much for feeling so furious. We were all angry and hurt for being forced to this drastic change in our lives. And we couldn't do anything about it but keep going. Our life consisted more of learning new surviving skills then enjoying and accepting life for what it was. She didn't want to open-up to any of her co-workers and share her life issues and burdens. She felt she couldn't trust anyone, she was afraid of people taking advantage of her still. But felt the need to share her thoughts and feelings with someone, anyone.

She had already lost more than one hundred pounds since my father's death. But we all Thank God she landed, what she later called "The best job in the world", at UTEP.

To our surprise, she began to adjust to her job quite well, as well as with the Students, Teachers and her Piers. After all, she had dedicated her entire life to cooking and cleaning our home and our Parish. It took her back to her comfort zone I suppose. All thought this was a bigger Institution, she loved making sure everything was done the right way.

She made work her second home. So now as a form of entertainment for us, she began to take us, to most of UTEP'S functions, rallies, football games and what ever games she was allowed to take us to for free and or at discounted price. We enjoyed every sport games, art shows and activities we attended, as long as we were close to her, and anything that resembled family fun. We all craved that family unity so much, that her co-workers began to help her out as much as they could. They'd break the rules for us sometimes by sneaking us in to functions she needed to pay for. Or they'd give her free tickets they weren't going to use. She began to build up her self esteem as well as her courage to know there were good people out their. We began to slowly see the silver lining in this new life. And it wasn't so bad anymore. We had our share of good times as well as bad times still, but we stuck together. We were learning to pull together instead of everyone doing there own thing. A co-worker advised her to apply for public housing which had not crossed her mind. And to our surprise she quickly qualified for a four bedroom, two bath apartment. Even though it was public housing and didn't live their long, we were ecstatic to once again claim our own bedroom.

We were now able to breathe better and learned to relax. We were all learning to stick together and becoming friends again. We were improving more and more every day, and even began attending church again. We were actually beginning to enjoy our spiritual community and being involved in some of the church activities. Time seemed to be going by quickly now as we were growing up, finished school and others completing trade schools. We graduated, fall in love, moved out and Marrying and had children of our own.

Chapter 11

My oldest sister moved back in town after separating from her boyfriend. She remarried and gave birth to another baby girl and was attending college. Even though my two youngest sisters were doing well in school, I wish they would have had more tender loving care from my mother like we did when we were young. Life was so simple when my father was alive. We had plenty of one on one time with both of them. They always managed to give us their undivided love, time and attention. Unfortunately my mom had forgotten that now, she was pre-occupied with working as much overtime as she could. So she was too busy and too tired to do anything fun with my younger sisters. She counted on us older girls to have them tag along with us as she now began to make her way to the single life of dating and going out with friends.

Was then when I married the man of my dreams, and thought I was going to spend the rest of my life with him. I met my husband at a club and it was love at first sight. We danced all night and saw each other almost ever weekend for about eight months. That was enough for us to decide we wanted to spend the rest of our lives together. In fact, my younger sister and I were going to have a double wedding. Unfortunately, my sister and her boyfriend decided to elope.

I had a beautiful church wedding in which I was two hours late too due to my mom's car broking down ha ha ha. Wow! We thought this has to be a sign of some kind. But I refused to have any negative thoughts and or remarks on this most wonderful day of my life. I wasn't going to allow that ruin my happiness. Fortunately my uncle, whom was to give me away, was right behind us so we jumped into his pick up and ran inside the church when we arrived. Thank goodness my husband and some of our guests were still waited for us. Sad to say not all my family members attend my wedding or the reception.

Not ever Lucy, the one that helped with my gorgeous white wedding gown and hairpiece. She volunteered to come help me dress that day, knowing I had other sisters that would want to assist me as well. But I felt honored to have her help me as well. My baby sister who was ten now was my flower girl and ring barrier. She looked so beautiful to me, like a little princess. It was a magical day for all of us.

As I looked at her walking up to me I couldn't help thinking that my father would have been very proud. I had bitter sweet emotions and shed tears of both happiness and emptiness I felt inside of me. A void that no one would ever fill and it hurt so much to remember him still. But I felt so proud to have being the first one of his daughters to get married. And to have had an official church ceremonial wedding just like he and my mother did. And I knew the others would some day have their wonderful wedding as well. I had always looked up to my parents as perfect in every way. They never argued, fought nor disagreed with each other. They were always smiling, laughing and making jokes. They were always happy so we had fun every single day.

They'd wait till we weren't with them or asleep so to discuss and/or resolve there "adult issues" as they put it. But they handled their family issues extremely well and in a civilized appropriate manner so to not overwhelm them selves or us. One of our family rules was that there was no excuse for hitting. They were totally against any kind of violence or abuse and that meant we'd be grounded if we would ever fight amongst each other. That day for me, marked the beginning of my blessed life with my now husband to have and to hold and love for the rest of my life.

I was so full of hopes and dreams, just like any other bride with so many expectations and thoughts of love and life with my husband. I was so excited that day, I felt like a true princess. My shoes were shinning, my eyes were sparkling, and my face was glowing as a happy tear ran down my cheek. I couldn't stop smiling and looking around, making sure everyone knew and understood that "I was getting married".

I looked around inside the church and look at all my sister smiling back at me. They looked like they were going to a grand ball in their beautiful gowns. The nuns had always told us that as long as we followed life and God's simple rules, we would be ok. "You go to school, do your choirs, grow up, fall in love, get married and we'd live happily ever after". I couldn't wait to have children and make my husband so happy too.

When I was getting out of the car and into the reception ball room, a car stopped in the middle of the street. A lady and her daughter got off and walked towards me. I thought they were guests but to my surprise. The lady said her little girl, who was about 3years old, wanted to give the bride a kiss, I felt so beautiful and special. My wedding reception was a blast, filled with people laughing and dancing and singing. The cake was a three tier white vanilla, strawberry filled cake, with very simple icing decorations. But we had two after parties that lasted two whole days after the wedding. We didn't begin our honeymoon till then since we had family and friends to attend too. When, we finally went home I realized that married life was going to be a new and exiting challenge for me. But I was ready to be as perfect as my parents had been together all their lives.

Till death do us part!

Chapter 12

Right!? Well that's not the way my life turned out at all. My husband and I moved into a studio apartment, which brought back unfortunate memories of the struggles we had after my father passed. Then I found out we happened to be surrounded by his family. His mother lived next door and his great grandfather lived directly across from us. And his cousins lived one on each side. Even though these accommodations were very uncomfortable for me, I didn't mind it much because I was so in love with him.

We had somewhat of a normal marriage at first, visiting friends and family and occasionally going to a movie or dancing which we both enjoyed. As long as I was with my husband, I was content. Besides, I knew other young married couples that also struggled at first, so I figured this was what they meant.

Unfortunately it was in our second year of marriage when we began to have marital problems. My husband still had personal challenge issues and was not a very good provider.

So I had to take up extra shifts at work to help him out.

But he'd now rather spend most of his time with his friends then family. As this situation progressed, I became more agitated and didn't want to put up with an absent husband. I didn't think it was appropriate for me to carry the marriage load by myself. I felt worse than if I were single because I hoped everyone knew I was now a married woman. I was saddened to know he'd rather be elsewhere. Although I was going through a rough time in my marriage, I enjoyed my family's company. My mom would bring my two youngest sisters over and let them hang out with me while she went out for the night. We'd watch movies, get burgers or flautas, which was their favorite foods and we'd stay up all night playing silly board games and telling stories. They loved staying with me so I wanted to move to a bigger apartment so I could have a spare room and fix it up real nice for them.

And so it was then when I became pregnant so I had come to definite decision once and for all. I asked him to change his irresponsible ways before the baby was born or I would leave him. Unfortunately he didn't change, in fact things got worse between us and I hardly ate during my pregnancy yet managed to gain about twelve pounds during my entire pregnancy. His parents and other family members as well as mine all had tried to reason with him to see if there was an ounce of hope in him. But nothing and no one seemed to be able to convince him to do so, not even me. I felt so devastated and didn't know what else to do.

So I had an extended talk with the priest in our church and needed guidance and the Lord's blessing to make my next move. I had to carefully assess our serious troubled situation as well as our marriage. I hoped for the same beautiful and loving environment for my daughter that I grew up in.

I gave birth to a healthy and beautiful six pound baby girl that wonderful morning, in mid May. I was only in labor about two hours and longing to have my husband by my side to share this my now happiest moment of my life. Unfortunately, he was out with his friends and never showed up at the hospital. But I thanked God for my baby and promised him I would give her the best life the Lord would allow me. I was disappointed that my husband came home very late the night I came home with my precious baby girl. I didn't care though; I was exited and grateful for my darling little girl. I knew I would teach her to be the loving, caring and respectful person my parents brought me up to be.

When my daughter was ten weeks old I confronted my husband with news of my request for a divorce. I was done with our marriage and was leaving him and all he said to me was. "You're not taking my brand new Stove"! Wow!

And here I worried he'd fight me for our only daughter, our new born baby girl. So, that was how I knew that we could stay with him no more, and

I would raise my baby all by myself. Why not? I thought to myself. My mother did a great job raising us.

I was shocked that he wasn't even willing to work out our differences because I knew he loved our daughter. He showed her so much love and when he was their and so did his entire family. But I feared that no one would care about her if I left. I knew he had grown up without a father himself. Unfortunately, his parents never married and didn't give him much guidance. So he didn't have any one to teach him good morals and values nor had good family traditions. So I guess I shouldn't expect much from him as a father to his daughter.

As far as I am concerned, he didn't deserve to have our precious little girl. She needed and deserved parents to love and protect her. I couldn't believe my husband refuse to grow up and be a father to his daughter, and the husband he promised me to be when we married. But I suppose that was the most he could give, and the way he was raised. And that was not a good life and future for my family, and it was a difficult and important decision to make but I had to leave my husband. And to this day, I am convinced it was the right thing to do, for everyone's sake.

Chapter 13

So there I was on my own, armed with my great memories of how my parents had raised me, and I was going to apply that to raising my own daughter. I faced the world head on with my head held high and the certainty that we would be alright. The first five years of my daughter's life, we moved around a lot to, California, Texas, Kansas and Illinois. I felt blessed as I landed grate jobs everywhere we moved to. I love to travel and having my daughter was no excuse for me not to fulfill my dreams, besides, she loved it too. But by the time we were back in Texas, my daughter had gone through numerous nannies, daycares and Pre-Schools at her young age. She has always been very well mannered and obedient as well as very mature for her age.

To my surprise, at her young age of five, she asked me if we could stay in this one place so she could go to the same school for the next six years or so because she can make friends. I was amazed at her idea and wasn't too sure I would stay in one place that long, but I agreed. So I got a job and rented a really cute apartment only a few blocks from her school. In fact, both the Elementary and Junior High School were right next to each other and only walking distance from our apartment.

I had to purchase new furniture, drapery, dishes all over again. There was a Daycare Center conveniently in the apartment complex that would transport her to and from school when needed. Since I tried to put in as much overtime at work as I could, and took a few courses at the community college, this accommodation was very convenient. All of the employees at the daycare facility were exceptional and friendly, courteous and professional and my daughter had so much fun and was very happy their too.

My daughter and I would go for walks after diner or ride our bikes she'd talk about all of her teachers and friends nonstop till we walked back. When we'd go swimming she loved for us to swim next to each other, because she said we were like Bambi and her Mother. I guess that is the way she viewed our relationship.

Shopping has always been her favorite and I don't think she's ever going to grow out of that hobby. I enjoy shopping with her because she's a blast to shop with. She not only chose her clothes, a purse, and shoes for herself, but she would find something for me too and the house, the car and sometimes even the neighbors too.

Funny, how I don't remember my mother ever taking me shopping by myself just her and me. My father would always take us all as a family grocery shopping and all other kinds of shopping too, clothes, shoes and toys. They'd both take us to all of our Doctor's appointments and school parent teacher meetings together. So I knew I wanted to be as loving and dedicated to my daughter just like them. I hope I live to see my grandchildren so I can spoil them as much as I have my daughter too or even more. That year I fell very ill and went to see my Doctor. He determined I had beginning signs of cancerous cells of some kind. And underwent a series of tests followed by biopsies then several surgeries to remove these cells but were only partially removed. These procedures were hurting my pocket book very hard.

I was attending fulltime at the local college but unfortunately dropped out of school that fall because I got so behind it wasn't even funny. By the time I wanted to catch up, it was virtually impossible. I now worked two full time jobs, therefore, longer hours just to keep up with the necessities. Things worked out pretty good for us for a while but I was wearing myself out. Life simply got too overwhelming for me as I was trying to balance both jobs, my daughter's school and her daycare functions as well as staying awake. I was not getting enough sleep. I even had to place the burden of waking me up on time for my next job on my daughter then had to drive her to my mom's house and get my night job. I'd get off work, go wake my daughter up and take her to school and I barely had enough time to go shower, change and off to my day job.

When I got out of that job I'd pick up my daughter from Daycare, feed her while I showered again and did laundry then put her in charge of my clothes while I slept. I hated to not see her but about a half an hour before and after I slept. I felt very exhausted, but couldn't complain, I loved my daughter and she was a pleasure to have. I had to work to keep food on the table and dress her but felt so exhausted. I was in a critical rollercoaster cycle and didn't know how to get out of it any more. I felt so tired both physically and mentally now that I had even developed stupid thoughts of taking her dad back just so he can help me with our financial responsibilities.

Then again, that was the reason I left him, he never helped me with child support so I was on my own. I cried so much and felt so guilty after having these thoughts. When I'd reach my work I'd be mad at myself for having such negative thoughts and automatically picture my precious baby girl. And I smiled at the image of her little giggling face in my mind. She'd make the rest of my shift worth working endless hours and would keep me going my entire life.

It was then when I stumbled upon the path of a man whom I thought I had fallen in love with and I thought he loved me too, but I once more made a terrible mistake. One night as I was constantly yawning at work, I was obviously noticeably tired. This man took the opportunity to introduce me to drugs. Drugs that made me forget I was tired but also made me forget my responsibilities as well as my sanity. Somehow this stupidity of mine lasted a few months. I loved the numbness feeling of it as if I didn't have a care in the world, but hated that it affected the people which I love with all my heart. I began to change and ironically I knew what the problem was but it was becoming an awful routine.

Chapter 14

As time went by, I realized this was more than I could handle and needed professional help. I knew I had to stop, I wanted to stop but I couldn't do it alone. I felt I was loosing control over my addiction but was in time to recover. So I turned to one of my sisters whom I had always had such a close relationship with, and confided in her and told her that my life had become very unmanageable and so insane because of my drug abuse.

After we cried in each other's arms, she said she'd help me get into a treatment center right away. She convinced me that I had to tell my mother. And I was so tired of hiding my problem and thought that no one knew about it. To my surprise, my entire family had there suspicions since we were so close. I hadn't even noticed that I had changed so much. See I began to leave my daughter at my mother's home for longer periods of time but was unaware of it. This was unusual behavior since I had always been an extremely dedicated mother, even thought I worked long hours. With my sister's support and by my side I was able to confront my mother with my embarrassing problem. They both helped find me treatment and I was admitted that same night.

The treatment center turned out to be of some help of course, but I guess I was expecting them to cure me for life. I was introduction to a twelve step program and hung on to that program staying clean and sober for about five years.

My daughter became a cheerleader for football team and was their a few seasons. And I found a grate job in which I could attend all of the games she cheered at, and I could make my twelve step meetings. We, ones more became a great inseparable team, her and I. My mom decided she would move in with us for a while. I had accepted a job at a Detoxification Center working as a Monitor Technician with women addicts attempting to kick their drug habits. At that time, I thought it was a perfect job for me since I was an addict in recovery myself and could help other people in their recovery as well. I would defiantly be a great asset for the company and I was.

My family was happy for me and said to be proud of my great progress, until my ex-boyfriend came back and charmed his way back into my life once more. My mother instantly moved out of my house and said she feared I would relapse. I assured her I wouldn't do that anymore since I knew it would only destroy my life. This left a bitter taste in my daughter's mouth since she knew that the relationship with my boyfriend had ruined our lives. But she accepted him since she didn't have much of a choice, and he always respected her as my daughter. I had always made our relationship clear to him when it came to my daughter. I was her mother and nobody had the right to neither discipline her nor give me advice when it came to her. And he always did respect that and never interfered in our mother-daughter relationship.

A few days later I relapse, just as everybody expected but it only lasted a few weeks. I then left him and moved to California to stay with my sister. Unfortunately we only stayed about three months, I should have stayed longer, I love my sister more than she'll ever know. I just don't have the gift of showing it, like her. We should have never come back. We should have never left her house. I have regretted that day so much.

When we returned to town, I began to work real hard again and it took me less than one month to move out of my Mom's house. Unfortunately I misplaced my daughter's school transcripts in the move, she was given a TASS Test in California and they sent her results to her new school. To our surprise, she mastered all of them and was promoted to High School to the Tenth Grade. I was so proud of her because she was the only thirteen year old at the time and in seventh grade but promoted to the tenth grade. That same day, I enrolled her at the High School and it was as frightening for me as it was for her. We were sitting in the office signing all the paperwork for her to begin the next day. Just then the school Nurse came in to take her to her office but as they reached the hallway, the bell rang, announcing a next class change. As soon as my poor little girl just thirteen years old and four feet, eight inches short found herself in the middle of a herd of tall strange kids. She ran back to me crying in my arms like a two year old would in a daycare.

That is one of my most precious moments!

Chapter 15

After closing the door for privacy I began to assure her that there were more kids her age. At that, the registrar told us that she was actually the youngest student at the school at the time. We went home and two days later she finally got the nerve to start her new school, and I couldn't be happier and prouder of her courage to face that fear of kids that were much older, bigger and taller than her.

Her teachers were amazed to know she was smarter than even most seniors in high school. I received compliments from office staff, teachers as well as other parents. But my daughter has always been the humble type and didn't like to take any praise from anyone, not even her teachers.

Just as we had settled in an apartment and money was a bit tight, I allowed my boyfriend to stay with me for a few days. He wanted to make our relationship work but I knew it was impossible for our drug use was inevitable when we were together. So the relationship was doomed from the moment we even looked at each other. Never the less I allowed him to stay a few days. I noticed his drug abuse was much more serious than mine had ever been in the past. We had gotten tickets that turned into warrants and I knew this relationship was getting me in deeper trouble.

I had gotten arrested because of him before and I wasn't going to allow that again. He got a job where I was working at, since he wanted to prove to me that he wasn't going to relapse anymore, or so he said. But it was clear to me that he was full of false promises. I moved on to a different job since I noticed he began his old ways of coming home extremely intoxicated again.

One day I came home from work and found him passed out instead of at work. He had done this three days in a row now, so I woke him up and told him I didn't want to do this any more and he had to leave. This lifestyle was rapid forming I noticed, and I refused to relapse ever again.

So I woke him up and told him to leave and to never come back to me again. Just before he left, I reminded him of what he had once read to me, while we read our twelve step literature. And he couldn't remember so I reminded him with tears in my eyes that the definition to the word "insane", is to repeat the same mistake over and over expecting a different result. It was then when I made the decision to never take him back. I had to be strong for my daughter. She deserved better than that, a fun loving mother again and for the rest of her beautiful life. I realized that it wasn't going to be easy at first but I had always pulled through by myself before and this was no different. I couldn't believe I had stooped that low. To fall for a drug addict and worse, become one, what was I thinking? I promised myself as well as my daughter, that I would never take him back.

My boyfriend and I had had an off and on relationship for many years and I loved him very much. It was going to be very difficult for me to re-adjust to being single again. The chemistry was defiantly their between us no doubt, but so was the drug abuse like routine to go with our names. Hence the relationship was ultimately doomed from the first day we moved in together.

He kept coming back to me and pleading and begged me to take him back, but I knew better now. I felt I learned from my mistakes and refused to fall into that cycle forming horrible lifestyle. I could never take him back ever again. It took me a few months of hard work to pick myself up again but I did it. I had a good feeling about moving forward now. I was slowly making amends with people I had hurt as I tried real hard to catch up with all the bills. My tickets of course were the hardest to keep up with since they were very expensive so I hadn't gotten around to all of them yet. I was being pulled over almost every time I left my house for work and given yet another ticket for no car insurance and or registration. I had decided that no matter how tight money was from now on. I was only going to work one job at a time so to not get overwhelmed.

So it was really tough for me to keep paying for all the tickets, my rent, food it was very stressful. But I tried a different and more productive approach to life and it had worked grate so far. My daughter seemed happier to know that I was working hard and so I even began going out on the weekends again. But I kept close to my entire family again and even closer to my daughter, which she loved. I had a boyfriend now and I loved that he despised drugs and wasn't much into clubbing. So we just visited each others home and spent a lot of time together.

My daughter approved of this man for me since his life only consisted of work home and me. He was very anti-social and didn't like to be around any particular crowd of people. He was just happy to spend time with me or us, my daughter and me, watching movies or having a cookout together which was a lot of fun.

Not everything was perfect but, I was proud of myself because I was doing much better than I had in years. I was doing a very good job despite of me using drugs in a more casual way now. I found out that I could control my drug use and so I used drugs as a recreational way now. I mean, didn't get wasted anymore but I knew my ex-boyfriend could never be able to handle it the way I did now. I only used once or twice a month and when I was out and away from everybody. And so it was then when I was out one night after work and was undecided were to go. I ended up driving to a local bar near the town I lived. As I drove up and, parked in front of the bar, I noticed two police cars across the street. And as I was walking inside the bar, I made eye contact with two officers, since they were staring at me from were they were. I didn't pay too much attention to them and went inside.

Chapter 16

The place was pretty empty so I found a few friends that were sitting up on the stage. They waived for me to sit with them and as I walked passed the owners. I asked why it was so lonely and they said that that maybe the cops outside were scaring them away, and we all laughed at their comment. I sat with my friends but only had one beer and left the second one half full. I left the place after about twenty minutes later, since I wasn't really having much fun and felt very uncomfortable.

Before I left my house that night I had a strange feeling in my stomach, but I couldn't quit make out what it was. Maybe it was my sixth sense, but I didn't listen and I know now that I should have. As I walking to my car, I noticed that the two officers standing across the street in front of their cars also getting into their cruisers.

But I got in my car and began to drive off towards my new boyfriend's house. Then I realized that a police cruiser followed me up the very dark street and turned his lights on signaling me to pull over, so I did. When he walked up to me I asked him why he had pulled me over, I knew I hadn't done anything, but he refused to tell me why he did. So I felt I could out smart him by giving him a wrong name, since I thought I had left my purse at home, or so I thought, besides he wasn't answering my questions either. Little did I know of what was to happen next?

The other police cruiser drove up behind the one right behind me and both officers talked a bit to each other then walked towards me. My heart began to beat faster as they approached me. They told me to step out of the car and I did. That night has ruined my entire life.

When he asked me if I was drunk, and I said no of coarse not I drank a beer and a half. Then I mentioned I was only in the bar for about twenty minutes and they saw me walk in and out, because they were parked in front of the bar the entire time I was inside. But they conducted a sobriety test on me anyway and I cooperated.

After discussing it with each other, I heard one ask the other what he should do next, being that I had passed the tests. After hearing this I stood there and waited. Thinking they had to let me go since I wasn't drunk. They walked towards me and handcuffed me anyway. After they read my rights and arrested me they walked me to the police cruiser. I asked them why I was being arrested and they totally ignored me. They searched my car without my permission and that made me real angry. But to my surprise, my purse was in the trunk of the car. I had totally forgotten that it was in there, and for the first time in my life I wished I had left it at home.

They looked through my purse, found my Driver's License and ran it through the system. They found out I had been in Jail for outstanding warrants a few months before and so they questioned me on my jail time, but I didn't think much of it. I told them I would answer all of their questions correctly. I figured they now knew I had been in jail and was embarrassed by it but I was sure they've seen worse. But instead of them doing their Jobs, they were having a ball looking through all of my Pictures that were inside of my purse.

They did mention my Driver's License was in my purse but my Photographs were much more exciting to them they said. I was very uncomfortable at them staring at me then back to the Photos. That was when I remembered that I had my photo album in their. I had taken professional pictures of myself the year before, and some were semi-nude photos of myself.

They talked amongst themselves as I sat handcuffed inside of the Police car. They came back telling me very casually, that they had called a tow truck to impound my car since the care was not registered in my name yet. I explained to them that I was giving payments on it so I couldn't register it until it was paid in full. So I asked them if I could call my mother or one of my sisters to come pick it up so it wouldn't be impounded. I knew it was going to be difficult for me to get the car out without the title not being under my name.

They said no and I was going to be taken to jail. When I asked them why I was being arrested, they said I had several outstanding warrants. Since I had been in jail in early January for more warrants, I believed them. I had no reason not to. After sitting inside the cruiser for about half an hour, they told me to call the person who sold me the car. When I did and he arrived we were given permission to talk and they didn't even ask him much. They were to busy chatting with each other. My friend was very upset and was considering taking the car back.

Chapter 17

I felt disappointed with myself but promised to pay his car off as soon as I could. We weren't sure what they were going to do to him either. He was pretty upset since they woke up at that time of night. We waited for the tow truck for well over an hour, but it never showed up. It was after one o'clock in the morning when they finally walked up to us and told my friend he was free to leave. He didn't even question what was going to happen to me or anything, he just left. I thought they were going to leave my car there and take me to jail.

After my friend was completely gone and out of sight, they told me to step out of the car, they took my handcuffs off. They told me get in my car and drive to the police station which was about a mile away. But one cruiser would drive in front of me and the other would drive behind me, "in case I wanted to drive away" one said. Since I had had an Evading Arrest charge in the past I thought, that was why we were driving that way, it must be there procedure or something. We arrived at the Station and they told me were to park. And I did just that, I was placed in a holding cell and they took my car keys away and handcuffed me again. I noticed they still had my pictures in there possession.

They were having fun smiling then glancing at me and flipping threw all of my pictures over and over again and making nasty comments. It was then when I began to feel extremely uncomfortable and nervous, but most of all, angry!

How dare they look through my personal photographs and look at me and make me feel like they were undressing me with there eyes. I immediately demanded they return my pictures back to me. They ignored me for a long time as I kept looking around the building and for signs of anyone else being in their, but I didn't see anyone. There was a video camera up on the corner and I was looking straight at it when one of the officers walked up to me and handed me my photo album. But he looked a bit disturbed, and told me that there cameras didn't work in the station. I asked him to take the cuffs off and surprisingly, he did.

I looked through my photos and noticed they didn't give them all back. They kept some of my semi-nude photographs, and I insisted they return them to me. But they just kept ignoring me and walked away. They both walked to the back of the small building and took what seemed like an hour, but really I think it was about half an hour. When they finally returned, they told me I had to cooperate with them in order for them not to take me to jail for my warrants and I could keep my car.

I then remembered that I was scheduled for surgery in two weeks. It was to be the last of my surgeries since the first time they had told me I had cervical cancer. Not to mention my daughter's fifteenth Birthday party the weekend after my surgery. So when they said they had a plan for me not to go to jail. Yes of course I wanted to hear it. But when one of them said "I would love to put my dick right between your breasts," with a devious smile on his face, I freaked!

I frowned in disbelieve at what I had just heard, and everything after that echoed as they continued to say what they wanted me to do to them. They kept describing many different sexual fantasies they'd want to practice on me as soon as possible. I inhaled a deep breathe and must have taken a long time to exhaled because I felt so light headed and felt nauseous with every word they said. Oh my God I was going to throw up.

I became scared stiff almost immediately thinking of what would happen to me if I would run as they opened the cell I was in. Fear took over me instantly and I knew I was defeated. I thought they'd shoot me in the back if I ran and probably say I tried to get away or something. I could scream at the top of my lungs, but if I screamed, I was doomed any way being that there was no one there but us. They could always, knock me unconscious and stuff something down my through. A million thoughts were racing through my head all at once.

Now I didn't want to come out of that cell, not until the morning when the world was awake and it was crawling with people here. Now I knew I had to play along and just somehow do what ever they told me to do. I felt I had no choice but to do what ever they told me to do.

Chapter 18

They told me they were going to let me out and I was going to follow them the same way we drove here, one cruiser in front of me and the other behind me. I started to take short breaths knowing they have planned something evil and conniving back there. Oh God, I thought to myself, where are they taking me? This didn't sound good at all, not for me anyway.

One Officer let me out of the holding cell and the other handed me my car keys back to me. I was instantly frightened beyond intimidated when they opened up the cell. My heart was racing and I wanted to scream in anticipation of not knowing where we were going or what they were going to do to me.

One of them told me to get in my car and follow him up passed the station to an isolated dirt road. I was unaware of any roads where they were taking me, and all I knew was that I needed to follow them and I did. I knew I was driving but I was still their prisoner. My fear was so intense that I couldn't see passed the hood of my car. I found myself praying as I trembled uncontrollably. It was so dark and scary out there, I never knew of any hidden road ever existing there. In fact I had never seen this place before.

Then they signaled me to park my car and as my car stopped so did my heart. They were in control and I needed to cooperate or they could set me up in so many ways if I tried to yell for help. The worse part of it is that the Chief of police, the mayor and the entire town would have believed there story, because they were cops. I was not given a choice to go free yet or to be dismissed. They just had a plan! Their plan and that was the only plan that mattered to them not I how I felt. I looked around and saw that it was a pitch black night and that's when a rush of fear washed over me.

When we arrived to what they seamed to have thought was the perfect spot, they told me to step out of the car and I did. I stood there staring at them for a while and felt I'd have a panic attach which I had never experienced before but I was extremely close now. But before I had a chance to let the fear set in, one of the Officers walked up to me and told me to perform oral sexual on both of them. He ordered me to do his partner first because he wanted to watch. Or else they were going to take me to the downtown jail for a very long time. I was afraid they'd add more charges to the once they said I already had.

I just stood their and knotted my head no in disbelieve and as I started to speak, they ignored me and as if had a mute button or something. No, this couldn't be happening to me, this was a mistake. They were kidding right? They were just trying to scare me so I wouldn't be out so late. That was it, this was just a plan to scare me, and it worked so could I go home now, I thought. But they weren't kidding and it was not a joke. I couldn't believe that "they" were telling me to do this.

I stood there, trying to understand what was going on, and thinking maybe I didn't hear them well. But they made it very clear, they weren't asking, they were telling me to "do them both". I knew I didn't want to go to jail of course but I couldn't help to feel sick to my stomach. I wanted to run, but was afraid they would shoot me and get away with it. I was still in their custody and had an evading arrest charge in my past so running away from them was out of the question.

I wasn't a bad person, why was this happening to me? Dare I kick them in the balls? I had always been strong enough to defend myself from any jerk that would ever try to hurt me or take advantage of me. But that confidence I felt I always had to protect myself, was now gone! For the first time in my life I felt so powerless over the situation I was in. I wasn't calling the shots. I felt I was being forced to do something I didn't want to do. It was the Police Officers that were calling the shots and were scaring me so much, I thought I would have a heart attach.

They were in total control of my body, their authority and their badge and they had guns. They just smiled at each other and place their hands on their "guns" I was now horribly scared and I started to breath heavily but softly and kept nodding my head "no" in disbelieve.

I didn't want to do this. Please don't make me do this, I thought, but couldn't say it. I certainly wasn't a teenager or a saint and have been with a man before of course, but not under these circumstances. Not against my own free will. Not without my consent and certainly not under intimidation and fear. How could they be telling me to perform such hideous acts? It was most frightening to me to know that I was been ridiculed and overpowered by police officers.

But they kept talking and laughing and grabbing themselves and finally, the bossier one pulled me towards him and pushed me down on my knees in front of his partner. He told me to put my cowboy hat on and do him first because he wanted to watch. It was then when my tears, without warning began automatically rolling down my face, nonstop. They were forcefully touching my entire body. The bossier one was grabbing me from behind and getting aroused by watching the other. I kept flinching not knowing if they were going to beat me or hit me from behind.

They kept touching their guns and my head so fiercely that I really believe they were going to shoot me on the head. My tears never stopped falling from my eyes but they didn't seem to care, and pretend to not notice. Didn't they realize I was not having fun? I thought to myself. When I was done with him I spit on the floor gagging as I attempted to throw up. It infuriated both of them so the bossier officer who was watching said it was "his turn now". He forewarned me not to spit with him "or else" he said. He then kept telling me to take my hat off then on again and grabbing my head not caring that he was pulling on my hair too.

Chapter 19

All the knowledge I had acquired throughout the years about violence and men dominating women against their will, was now gone. I was defeated and they had won. They were in charge and I was at their mercy and I was still praying for a fucken Miracle.

I felt a mixture of fury, shame and horror but mostly, overcome with fear still. I was so helpless and alone and I couldn't even call the Police because, they were the police as well as my Attackers. I found myself blaming God once more for permitting so much horror in my life. But God must have been listening to me that night as I prayed for a miracle for some super hero to jump out of nowhere and rescue me.

I remember a man walking up towards us from the other side of a fence which I hadn't even noticed was there. I was trying to focus through my tears as he walked closer, but when he saw the two Police cruisers, he turned back real fast and left. I wanted to yell out for him to come back, but was too afraid of what the Officers would have done to me or him if I would have scream for help. I felt numb, disgusted and angry. As the officers were distracted by the man, I got up, took a few steps to my car and spit inside my car and grossly into my cowboy hat. Then as I watched as that man walk away, so did my hope of being rescued out of the misery I had just been put through.

To this day and at that moment, I believe that if it weren't for that man that saw the two police cars and officers and a regular car, they would have killed me and nobody would have known who had done it. Nobody would have suspected the two Police Officers had used and abused me, a woman with a criminal background that had just gotten out of jail three months before.

After I had done what they had told me to do to them, I didn't want them to get even angrier with me as they seemed to be. They still wanted more, I can hear it in there voice. I didn't want them to book me in jail after being their sex slave for the night. They took the ticket they had written up for me with a list of violations which I was unaware of. And one of them tore it in half. He gave me one half and kept the other half but I didn't even look at it. They took the License Plates from my car and gave me a phone number to call to find out what day I was to pick it up. They then told me "we know where you live and so you better not say anything to any one, not like they'd believe a woman with your background anyway". I didn't care; I just wanted to leave. As I was driving away I swear I couldn't even see straight from the tears that seem to have a mind of their own. I felt disgusted, nauseous, and drained! How could two Professional Police Officers so well educated and well respected by the community had been so vulgar? They used their authority to intimidate me and used my past criminal history against me to gratify their sexual needs. I wonder if they know I wanted to go home and die that night!?

As I was driving home I detoured to my mother's house and hope of finding the courage to tell her what had just happened to me. I just wanted her to hold me. I wanted her to hug me tight. I wanted her to wrap her arms around me and rock me to sleep and make the pain and sadness I felt, go away. I remembered earlier when I dropped my daughter off at my mother's house. She smiled at me then kissed my cheek softly and said "goodbye sweetie and please be careful" then gave me her blessing.

When I told her that I was probably going to spend the night at my boyfriend's house she said "maybe it's better dear, this way you won't be driving at night where something bad can happen to you". It hurts to picture my mother saying this to me now. With a gentile smile on her face as she gives me a kiss on the cheek like she did when I was a little girl.

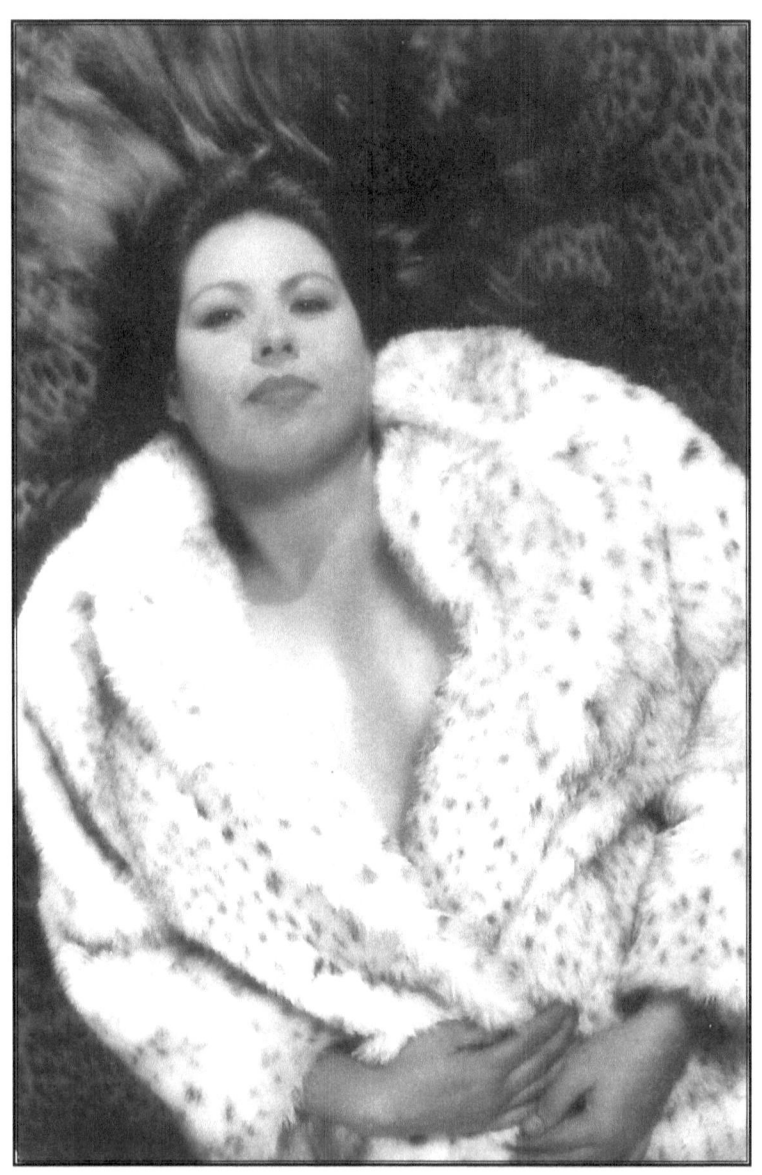

Chapter 20

When I reached her house, I went into her room. I was still sobbing and shaking, thinking weather to wake her up or not. But I couldn't, I just couldn't bring myself to share this horror I felt with anyone. It was selfish of me to share this pain, shame and devastation I felt, with yet more innocent people, especially my mother who was sleeping so comfortably in her bed. It wasn't fair to wake anyone up to see how awful I looked and felt. I thought you could see right through my pain. I thought it was noticeable enough to where they might feel the horror and it wasn't fair, it wasn't their fault. But I didn't feel it was my fault either and I hurt, I hurt so much. I slowly dragged myself into the shower as if I weighed two thousand pounds. I wanted to get all the filth out of my body and mind. I wanted it all to go away and was crying again uncontrollably and couldn't stop. I washed my mouth out with soap so hard it felt numb for a long time. I scrubbed my body till it was red and I thought and I thought I would bleed. I cried so much my eyes were so swollen I couldn't see any more. I must have under the water for at least a few hours. The hot water had way passed gotten cold. I was freezing as I just sat inside the shower crying and thinking I should have gotten to jail. They should have done their job and taken me to jail. I felt devastated and still couldn't stop crying.

I shouldn't have gone out that night! Why didn't I listen to my gut feeling? Why didn't I ever listen to my Mother? Well it was too late now and I just wanted this night to be over with. Oh god would any one really miss me if died tonight? I thought? I just wanted to die!

But what about my daughter and my mother oh no what was I thinking, I had so much family that loved me that I couldn't die, not like this, not for this. This hurt worse than any surgery I had ever had. I had been crying for about three hours under the now cold running water, but had lost tract time. My mother finally woke up knocked on the door and asked me if I was all right. But I found I couldn't break her heart. Where would I start and could she help erase this humiliation I felt? No, No one could ease the pain I felt.

I just couldn't bring myself to tell her. Besides the Officers told me they knew where I lived, and they told me not to tell anyone. "No one would believe you or even care, not with your record!" they said. The next few weeks, my stomach felt empty and hollow from throwing up so much. I felt so nauseous I couldn't eat. And no, I didn't dare tell anyone about that night for fear of the officers coming back to take me into custody again or worse, this time disappearing me for good. I turned to isolation, and was plagued with depression and not letting my daughter out of my sight. I completely stopped going out, had no social, family or spiritual life. Didn't even go grocery shopping or any kind of shopping, I made up excuses and sent my daughter or took her along with me.

I was frightened of these jerks and was loosing it completely. In the next following weeks after this, I lost my job, my car, lost our apartment along with our furniture. I lost all of my daughter's childhood memorabilia which she never forgave me for but worst of all, I lost me!

I noticed everything startled me now and developed panic attaches. I lived in this panic state of mind thinking they'd come back and use me again. I feared they would after me and shut me up permanently this time so I would tell. So I moved into a little one bedroom unfinished one bedroom house my mom had next to her house. We'd have to share the yard with my oldest sister and her family, whom all lived with my mom. But I didn't care. I just wanted to be close to my family and feel at least a little bit of protection, for I lived in constant fear. They had about a hundred dogs, seemed like, and they barked at anybody walking by and attacked any cats or dogs that would dare come inside the fence. So I knew no one could just walk in of even dare to try.

So I wanted to live their even if it meant to do without certain necessities, as long as we were safe. I knew my daughter didn't understand what was going on but I needed to feel safe. My family had doubts about me relapsing again maybe. But I knew that nothing was as bad as what I had gone through and the way I felt.

I was falling deeper in my depression. I had become a person, without a personality or a sense of humor. My daughter even accused me of becoming a lonely, angry and bitter person. At times it'd run into some male chauvinist man make a stupid remark about a girl. And I'd catch myself taking it extremely personal now. As when before, I'd maybe see a joke they were trying to tell.

I couldn't help feeling anxious and sad all the time, with nothing to look forward to any more. I decline all dating invitations. I found something wrong with every man I met, and or suspicious of whether he's a predator or a rapist. I didn't feel I belonged anywhere I went, and couldn't fit in anyone. Not at work, when I worked, not with friends or my own family, much less people I didn't know.

Chapter 21

I kept my guard up and had created this shield around me which forbid me to get close to any one and vice versa. I felt nervous and extremely uncomfortable wherever I was at. I began to think that every man was as had this beastly way of thinking. Some times I couldn't even stand myself so I decline all invitations because I didn't want to ruin there fun.

My sisters worried about me as I turned down their invite to cookouts, birthday parties or just hang out with them. When I did accept the invite I just sat there distant and looking right passed them the entire.

They accused me of been so negative and making hasty remarks at most of their conversations. But it pains me to laugh, and when I look up at them and see them laugh, I always wonder if they're laughing at me if I would tell them what happened to me and what I was going through. Would they loose respect for me? Would any body loose respect for me? Would they blame me for being out so late? Would they dare think "that's what I deserved"? They knew I was the toughest one in my family and I could handle anything and anyone. I didn't know how I had allowed myself to be put in this predicament. I didn't know how to bring it up. I didn't know how to tell them that I felt weak and was hurting and it was eating me up inside.

I couldn't find a suitable conversation in which to join into when I was with them anymore. Sometimes I just wished they'd just stop talking to me and leave me alone. But I didn't want them to leave me alone, they just didn't know that. I needed them so much. I needed someone to tell me that I was safe, even if I didn't feel safe.

They'd always been there for me, every time I cried, every time I need them and every time I was scared. But it was different now, I had an awful secrete that was poisoning me from the inside out and reflecting on my entire being. Didn't they notice the difference in me? And why wasn't anyone helping me? Why didn't they ask me what was wrong or if I needed help as if they could read my thoughts. I wish I could have expressed my love and hate and anguish with my family and friend again like before, when I didn't have this horrible secrete. But I was afraid to trust any body any more. Some people still believe that victims are the instigators, and they deserve what ever happens to them. Others disguise words so to not say it was completely your fault. "You deserve what you got because of the way you lived your life." & nbsp;

If I could just lie down and sleep, just be alone and sleep, without having to talk to anyone or leave my house I'd be fine just fine! Nothing interests me anymore and my future plans or goals had been chattered in a million irreplaceable pieces.

I'd give anything to feel as safe as when my father lived. I never worried about my safety when he was alive.

 Oh God I couldn't stand to feel this hatred towards anyone, I wasn't taught to hate anyone. But I do hate what these men did to me!!!

I do hate them so...Yes that's got to be it, I do hate them!

Over a year and a half had passed by. I was working again but we still lived in the little house next to my sister. My daughter wasn't in high school any more but was working and attending college. The unavoidable was now happening. My daughter was growing up and going out with her friends. I had kept my daughter as close to me for as long as I could. Sometimes her friends would pick her up and bring her back home when they hung out together or went out.

I cried from the time she left the house, to the time she came home. I worried that they would get pulled over and they'd take advantage of her or her friends since they were so young, and even more vulnerable than me. She now had a driver's license and a car but she'd always call me before she would leave her work place or school. And I would time her and would literally stare at the clock and the window till she arrived at home.

Chapter 22

One September night my daughter came home after hanging out with friends, and I had fallen asleep but woke up startled as she walked in. I remember being so angry at myself for falling asleep instead of waiting up for her as usual. We sat on the bed and she began talking to me about her night out. I loved having girl talks with my daughter. And we laughed as she shared her adventure with her friends. I had always made sure I kept an open mind and be there for my daughter without being judgmental no matter what she told me. I passed on all the morals and values my parents brought me up with and allowed her to be herself around me as well. I always told her to call me if her or her friends had drank or unable to drive home. I assured her I would never question or be angry with her for calling me as long as she was safe. Thank god she did always trust me and never take advantage of this. She did casually drink with her friends as most teenagers do, but she never abused alcohol or my trust in her. If I would have told her never to drink alcohol she probably would have done the opposite, I think. She did call me in several occasions when her friends would drive and were unable to drive and I would pick them up and take them home as well. Their parents understood and were grateful I would bring them home.

One of her friends had bought a car and took them for a cruise. She then, casually said to me "oh yea mom and on the way home two blocks away from here we were pulled over".

And before she could continue I just freaked! I grabbed her arm and literally lost it. I began shaking her back and forward and wanted to know exactly what had happened to her. I wanted to know what they had done to her. I was hysterical and couldn't keep talking any more! I let go of her and realizing what I was doing to her. And put my hands on my face as my tears just came pouring down uncontrollably like water from an open faucet.

She saw the terror and hurt in my eyes as she took a minute to grasp the fact that something was horribly wrong with me. She held me in her small arms as she let me cry it all out and she cried because she knew it was something awful but feared it was nothing I'd ever gone through. "Oh mom, it's ok just let it out" she said to me.

I was so tired of keeping this horrific secret inside me that my pain just oozed out of me with every breathe I took. My cried almost as much as I did that same awful night. My poor daughter hugged me as tight as she could again then she pulled me back gently, looking into my still aching eyes. And finally asked me, what had happened to me, she needed to know everything from the beginning.

And I just couldn't hold it in any longer, I needed to release this awful secret that was eating me up inside like a virus that had infected me entirely. What these two jerks did to me was destroying my entire heart, body and my mind. It was controlling my brain, and was dragging my self-esteem down lower every waking day. This was beyond my level of control now. At times I felt I was unable to think for myself, and didn't want to leave the house any more, not even for work. I was frightened they'd follow me or look for me and make me do those horrible and sick acts again. But I was more exhausted than anything and was ready to surrender. I needed to get out of this awful prison lifestyle I had placed myself in.

My daughter was only sixteen years old at the time. She first of all assured me that nothing like this had ever happened to her before and I absolutely needed to know this to feel at ease for her. Then she told me that I needed to report these officers as soon as possible. My daughter has always been mature for her age, but this is definitely something I'd never wanted her to here from her own mother's voice.

It hurt me deeply to tell her the discussing details of how these men humiliated me, so I didn't. They stumped all over my pride as a woman and a strong mother who would stop at nothing to defend her daughter. I didn't want her or anyone else to think less of me because of what had happened to me. I had always been tough and fearless, now I felt I couldn't even protect myself, much less her. I was supposed to always be there for her not the other way around. But she became my only solid rock and comfort. I apologized to her for all the grief I had put her through but if I would have known this was going to happen to me and affect me this hard I would have never gone out that night.

I love my daughter and life itself I always had, but at that point in time, I wanted her to leave me behind and just keep going without me. I cried so much you'd figure I'd run out of tears but I didn't. But I promised her I'd go the following day and speak with someone.

Chapter 23

The next day, that September morning 2003, I made an appointment with the Sheriff's Department. When I arrived I drove up and sat in my car for a while, to clear my head. But I quickly reminded myself that I did not want these officers anywhere near my daughter. And that gave me the courage to press charges on them. I wanted to get these two offenders off of the streets so I maybe I could sleep better knowing they wouldn't hurt my daughter or me.

I took a deep breath and got out of my car and somehow a million thoughts began to swirl into my mind. Before allowing anymore negative thoughts or feelings in my mind, I walked in. There was no turning back now. When I first walked in I felt this negative energy coming from the people there. When I commenced my statement it was very uncomfortable of course, since there were a group of people huddled in front of me to listen in. They began their investigation by asking me a series of questions. Made me feel that I was being treated as if it was in some way my fault for being out their in the middle of the night. I found I scare easier now when I feel cornered or pressured.

Both, The Sheriff's department and the Federal Bureau of Investigation conducted their investigations. I didn't feel comfortable talking about that night and what the Officers had made me do to a bunch of other officers. I kept thinking that these were also Law Enforcement Officers and that they might protect their own kind instead of me.

I was skeptical and couldn't just come out and tell them every thing these

Officers did and said to me. It was too embarrassing for me and so I held back a lot of details that day for fear they'd retaliate or go let the officers know I had told someone and come after me. I felt uncomfortable and particularly embarrassed to mention what they had put me through since I knew one of the sheriffs their. Although this sheriff and everyone their, were doing their job in a very professional manner. I couldn't ignore the way I felt because of the way I had been mistreated and stepped on by other officers. I was extremely nervous and told them my entire life story without it being a part of that night. Afterwards I thought they had communication with them and they'd somehow come hurt me in the middle of the night or something right after they'd find out I had broken my silence.

I knew these officers wanted me to tell them as much as possible but I didn't know how important it was to do so. I had no faith in any one of them anymore. In my book, they were all the same. I took a polygraph test and passed with flying colors of coarse.

During their investigation they asked me all kinds of the different unpleasant and unnerving question like, why hadn't I come forward sooner? Where they circumcised or not? They asked if there penis was big or small in size, thick or thin? If they had any particular scars, moles or tattoos? Were these men's privates shaved or not? As if I had night vision, I though. It was pitch black, I don't even remember seen the moon out that night, much less a tattoo on them. But they just kept throwing questions out their. They asked me if anyone witnessed this incident.

And then I remembered! Things started coming back to me. I remembered the man that walked towards us then left as he saw the police cars there. I told them how I really didn't even get to see his face though, being that it was so dark out and I was so nauseous and felt nauseous. I had to spit all over the inside of my car without them noticing so to not get them angrier.

Then there was a long silence in the room as they all looked at each other then smiled like if I had gotten something right. I looked up at them and asked. "What"?! One of the sheriffs promptly asked me if I still had that car. And when I said no, they all just slouched in disappointment. When I asked "why"? And he said because there might still be DNA in there. So they asked me if I could get it back and I said no. But I kept the cowboy hat in which most of the discussing stuff was still their, I just had to look for it. I also remembered that the bossier officer had mentioned to his partner that he was going to be married soon and all I could think of was. She didn't know what she was getting herself into.

Well after about four hours, they finally said they had something to go on. I went home and came back with hat and turned it into them and that was it. They began an investigation to see if they had done this before to anyone else. It scared me to think they might have done this to other women. I hadn't even thought of any other girls but my daughter, up until that day.

I must say I was impressed and surprised after we were done and I was told I could leave. They called me back to reassure me they would help me in any way they could. They ended the call by apologizing for what these officers had put me through. Even though I was still a bit shaken up, I had thoughts of taking my daughter and moving as far away as I could. But then a tiny drop of hope was buried deep in my heart and somehow kicked in and made me change my mind.

Two months later, on Thanks Giving morning, my daughter had gotten a turkey for me to cook. Cooking had always been a fascinating hobby for me and I loved cooking on the holidays. Only this year for me was sadly different for me. She wanted me to cook for her a delicious family meal which I had done since she could remember. So she had invited our entire family to our house for dinner but hadn't told me until that morning when she asked me to get up and cook. I could have slapped her for that not so pleasant surprise, since all I wanted to do was sleep all day on my couch just as I had been doing for the past nineteen months. I forced myself to enjoy the entire day, for her sake, but I do thank her for helping me so much.

Chapter 24

That December 2003 my daughter told me she was going to attend a spiritual retreat my sister had invited her to. I was ok with it as long as I could be alone with the misery dwelling in that awful routine depression that I couldn't snap out of.

That weekend she was away at the retreat, a friend of mine stopped by to see how we were doing. He stayed a while trying to convince me to hangout with him the next few days since my daughter was away and he didn't want to go home to his wife. We had been friends since my daughter was a baby. And he reminded me that he only married his wife because he didn't want to hurt her feelings since she had wanted to marry him since they were young. But I turned him down and told him to go home to his family anyway because I wanted to be alone. Before he left he use the restroom and was in there for a long time, when I asked him if he was ok, he said yes then walked out quickly and left.

I didn't notice anything strange until I went to the restroom and saw he had left a small pouch and I picked it up. I realized it was a small mount of my ex-drug of choice. I had been clean from drugs and alcohol for about two years. So I was confused and didn't know if my friend had forgotten it or left it behind on purpose for me, knowing I was going be stay clean no matter what. Well I decided to go for it and not let it go to waste. But to my surprise I began to cry like a baby and walked outside and threw it away instead. For the first time in years, I felt so relieved at having the will power to actually saying no to drugs. I chose to not use drugs that night nor any night any more.

When I picked my daughter up that Sunday night, she had a huge noticeably glowing aura around her, and she looked so peaceful and had this huge smiled on her face the entire way home. She even made me feel a bit of what she said she lived and felt at the retreat. She began telling me about how God had saved her and forgave her and then she turned to me and asked me to forgive her for the times she had doubted me, judged me, hurt me and that she loved me so much.

Even though I didn't quit understand her, and didn't know she was judgmental, I said ok and she just couldn't stop talking about how it was all going to be alright for us in the future, she said God promised her and us, that and more. You see, I guess that when I lost my faith in God, I forgot how wonderful He really is. So I wanted to feel what my daughter was talking about. Coincidently there was a retreat for adults the following weekend. Great, I said with a side of sarcasm. Without excuses but hesitating a little, I attended all three days and maybe because I was morally drained, felt defeated and so emotionally disturbed. I decided to give God another chance to come into my life again to see if He could maybe in some way make a change in me because I was already tired of caring this baggage full of anger, resentment and fear that had turned into hate.

Well like a slap in the face, I was astonished to have felt such a spiritual love I had longed for. But most of all, the unbelievable peace that came over me was extremely overwhelming. There was this room full of praise and people glorifying God that I had never seen in my entire life before, except in other religions. I never knew this kind of worship existed in our own catholic community.

We never worshiped God that way when I was in private school. But I liked this new way of worship, this brought a sense of soothing forgiveness into my heart. I asked God to forgive me for the way I felt about these men, I so wanted to leave absolutely every bit of negativity there and take with me only all the good I needed. There were also so many community activities amongst the church that I signed up for immediately after the retreat.

So I immediately began attending as many Bible classes as I could and even joined the choir were I was happy to be a part of since I love to sing. I became very grateful to God that I saw it as an obligation to serve him for the rest of my life. They found it funny but not ridiculous when I told them that I wanted to be a nun when I was a little girl. And I think I probably would have if we would have stayed in Chicago, maybe.

Chapter 25

For the next few years, I practically lived at the church. I sang at retreats and helped others see the light as I saw it was my new way of life. I attended spiritual seminars and groups as well as singing at different church functions.

On December 19, 2003 I received a phone call from the Sheriff's office. They said they had finally completed their investigation and had taken these officers into custody and were arrested. They wanted to inform me that the Officers were no longer Law Enforcement Officers but regular civilians. They said they had stripped them of their uniforms and there badges. It took them a while to realize what I already knew, but thank god they had understood that these people weren't fit to be cops.

I broke down and cried for a few hours as a blanket of relieved fell over me, to know that they were finely off the streets. My daughter and other women were not going to be taken advantage of by these two poor excuses of men any more.

When there arrests was made public it was all over our local stations and news paper headlines and there was a number to call for women to come forward if these officers had violated others too in the same or similar situation. A few days later a woman called in and reported that a similar incident had happened to her involving one of these officers. But this was only the beginning.

I was then advised to seek professional help and counseling and just casually threw in there that I could pursue this case with a civil suite. I was then amazed to learn that they were only charged with Civil Rights Violation of a woman in custody and served less than four hours in jail. No wonder they advised me what they did. After their release, I was astonished with disbelieve, and knew I wanted to do more to make people understand the seriousness of what they had done to me.

Our system constantly tells us we need to report a crime and or rape as soon as it happens. There are different kinds of rape and it affects every one differently. But you must report every crime as soon as possible. They kept reassuring me I had done the right thing and how brave I was for doing so. These men knew they did wrong and therefore had no choice but to plead guilty.

Unfortunately for me, that wasn't enough. I felt I had unleashed some very angry demons and they weren't too happy I had broken my silence. And I don't just mean the officers.

I was introduced to the victim's assistance program that was available and was advised to use their resources to get counseling. But I was only awarded six months worth of service. I did give it a try since I now felt anger in addition to my still feeling depressed again.

Unfortunately, my therapist whom is a psychologist was a joke to me at the time. I couldn't help thinking I was awarded six months word of therapy so I had to hurry up and feel better fast. I couldn't concentrate and I now felt that my mental state of mind was slowly deteriorating. In fact I was getting worse right under his care and I felt he didn't even notice my massive depression had now progressed even more.

He too, like the officer's was an educated man whom could one day try to outsmart me, was the way I saw him. I don't think he ever realized I had that aspect of him. He never asked for me to give him specific details of that humiliating night I felt was hunting my present and ruining my future. He could have tried to help me cope with my embarrassing memories and recurring nightmares that were getting worse.

Instead, he said he wanted to perform hypnosis on me, and as expected of coarse, I declined! As if I would ever allow any man any where near me while I was asleep, unconscious and vulnerable. As a professional he should have known better than to ever suggest that to me. I was diagnosed with Post Traumatic Stress Disorder as if that was supposed to mean much to me. A title attached to my feeling like crap, how nice. I'm afraid I'm still waiting for the cure.

He started me on depression medication which I took but found there was neither a magic pill to make me feel better, nor a special tool that can fix what they've destroyed in me. This was going to be a bump ride.

One day he suggested for me to go out again to a bar or a club by myself. Right! I mean, hadn't he been listening to me all this time? Didn't he know there were cops out their just waiting to take advantage of women! What part of the sight of a cop car would send me in to a frenzy didn't he understand yet? I saw these men's faces in every officer driving by. I was now convinced that this psychiatrist had no idea how I felt either, I was agitated upon arriving to his office every time and he didn't even notice.

He'd then repeatedly ask if I had any suicide thoughts and it was a bother since I figured, if he still hadn't figured out what was really in my mind. Then if I was suicidal, not that I was, but he never would have guessed that either. He may be a good therapist no doubt, but he could have sent me perhaps to a more adequate specialist female therapist since I was there for my health. I don't think my sessions with ended in a successful recovery at all.

I don't know what my therapist report read at the end of our session or what the outcome he thought I reached. But I wish he would have discussed it with me or helped me get more assistance from the state. He was a nice man but that was not enough for me because I needed professional help and my time was up and I didn't receive what I was so much in need of. Help!

Chapter 26

I discovered he uncovered a mesh full of feelings that were bottled up inside me and was left just hanging there to deal with on my own. I was unprepared to deal with my past, again. I didn't know how to handle my now opened up emotions and once more I became an immobile wreck. I had developed massive anxiety attacks as well panic attacks that were totally unpredictable.

My self esteem had dropped way below the lowest measurable level and I had purposely gained so much weighed for fear of anyone looking at me as a sexual object. When I finally realized how unhealthy I was, I knew I needed help again. This rollercoaster ride full of nothing but negative thoughts, emotions and feeling was holding me back from moving forward.

This psychologist assured me that I wasn't broken as I felt, so he obviously didn't understand me at all! Oh, but he's a man with several degrees to back up his expertise up in cases like mine, he said. So I don't understand why his expertise didn't work on me.

I found myself remembering a therapist my daughter saw once and as a child and she came to enjoy her visits. She treated her like a friend rather than a counselor. When my daughter was about five years old and wanted answers about why her Father and I were not together, I couldn't make her understand. So I took her to a child counseling service and she enjoyed talking to her therapist. I guess she must have been good at what she did because my daughter learned a lot from her and applied the advice that she'd give her. It did work out for both of us I suppose.

A few years later, the therapist was offered another job elsewhere so she told my daughter she wasn't going to see her any more, but would leave someone else in her place that she thought was as competent. My daughter was upset but understood this was a change she needed to accept and move on. She tried to talk to the other therapist but we both agreed she was not good enough and we felt we were fine now. We learned to except life as it came, and to deal with our own problems as they occurred, by ourselves. Sometimes it's better that way. I think! This therapist was truly one in a million. She helped my daughter and me both with our issues. Unfortunately for both of us, we will never find anyone like her to guild us through the recovery we need. I wished I would have found someone like her to have been there for me. We could have used some one like her then.

I was trying real hard to let go and let god, but it wasn't long before I found myself once more battling with what I called, "My Own Demons" again. I couldn't figure out why I was falling into this horrible depression again and couldn't shake it off?

Why couldn't I just get past this, why? What did I have to do to make it all better? I use to be as strong as my mother for my daughter. Now, I felt like I was sitting in the back seat of my own car and couldn't even give or receive simple directions from the back seat. Why would a person hurt another this much? It was no use. I couldn't understand it no matter how hard I tried. I'd sit there and cry till I was drained and exhausted and once again wonder, why? Why did this have to happen to me?

I have always been the strong one in my family and I didn't want these two jerks to continue ruining my entire life. I had a visit from my sister and said she was very worried about me. She didn't think it was fair for me to have to live my life as if it was going to be over soon. She and my daughter began giving me reasons why they looked up to me so much, and as they did I thought back to all the great times we've had together.

We told story after story and laughed at all the funny, crazy and weird things we had done in the past. Oddly enough my family members called on me when they needed some one to argue for them all the time. They'd tease me and bugged me to become a Lawyer of some kind. And believe it of not I should have become an Attorney, I think I would be a good lawyer. I had always defended myself and protected the rest of my family.

My sister then reminded me of an incident at the movies. We were sitting in the lower part of the theater and there were a group of about ten young men right above us. They were laughing to loud and were annoyingly walking in and out, which made it impossible to enjoy the movie. I got up for more popcorn, I Love popcorn, and when I came back and sat down. The manager walked up to me and said that someone had complained that we were been too loud. I couldn't believe he thought it was us. I explained to him that it wasn't us, but when he still didn't believe me I got upset at him and raised my voice to him. I got up and told my sister and my daughter to get up because we were leaving the guys that were making so much noise. Started laughing and I said "you see, they're the once making all that noise not us"

I was so angry I told my daughter and sister to get up because we were leaving. But when I looked to them, they were already walking out.

They were so afraid those guys would come after us, because they were escorted out of the building. But I was more angry than scared and felt I could fight them if I had to. Besides, I was right! Maybe it was foolish on my part, but I wasn't scared to stand up to any of them. We laughed at the memory and then I realized that she was right. I was living my life as if I had a terminally illness just waiting to die. My aches had gotten so ridiculous and physically painfully that I had even gone to a mental health program to seek help and wanted to file for disability because I was physically dragging myself through life now. This program assigned me a doctor that placed me on anti-depressant medication as well as medication for anxiety attaches which had gotten worse. They also assigned me to therapy sessions in which I have to say were of most help to me than the psychiatrist the state paid for, in vein.

With this program I paid a fee according to my income but it was well worth every penny of it. Although nothing seemed to cure my severely damaged soul and I struggled to recover a semi-normal life again. I felt there was hope and compassionate people here whom really helped me tremendously. They understood that I felt broken and ruined and were willing to help me at my own pace. I was trying to be happy, I had tried to be brave and had even tried to forgive them, but the harder I tried the angrier I became. I had tried to seek God because I still had had faith, but it kept getting harder to believe they made an awful mistake.

Truly everybody makes mistakes and we can not go back and change the past. And I admit that I've done things in the past that I'm not so proud of. But those are things I did, not who I am. But because this was not the first time these Officers had done this. I believe that this is who they are, and not some stupid mistake they made. They knew perfectly well what they were doing. I asked for strength to forgive them, but I couldn't. I really couldn't. I was thirty-five years old and certainly not a virgin when this happened to me. But I know that I didn't deserve what they did to me. They didn't have the right to take my perfect self-esteem away from me or my happiness. I had forgotten how to smile, and didn't care to look forward towards tomorrow anymore.

I had many dreams and expectations of the future just like every one else but now I felt I was in a coffin ready to be laid to rest. I felt that absolutely no one out there understood how I felt. How could they take my sunshine away? How did I allow them to invade me in every way possible? I didn't understand and I was tired of having more questions than answers. I thought that by now my daughter and I would be sharing stories about her college and arguing about the dishes. We'd be planning that trip to Disney World that we have always talked about ever since she was five years old. We added Las Vegas to our future mother/daughter trip since we have never visited neither of these two places. I didn't want to take her as a child because she would have forgotten the fun she'd have. So I wanted her to be able to enjoy both as much as I would.

Never in a million years did I ever imagine that this is how my dreams of the future would end up? If I live to be one hundred, I will never understand how I allowed for these two Officers to have robbed me of my life. This has left my past completely broken, my present totally vague and my future well, just, Empty!

Chapter 27

I was so tire of just existing and walking threw life like a zombie. With a vague expression on my face, I looked but couldn't see, I heard voices but couldn't listen, I listened but I couldn't comprehend. I had become accustomed to sleeping on the couch three to four hours a night, instead of having my eight hours of sleep on my bed!

I would have given anything to be half the person I use to be, so vibrant, funny and confident. My life was full of spunk that included a sexual and a spiritual life. I missed having a social life, going to the pool, bike riding, enjoying a good movie and shopping. I'd laugh at any thing and made every one laugh too, because I felt so happy and alive. I use to wake up with a great big smile, listened to music and sang out loud, not caring how I sounded to anyone.

I made the decision to force myself to do what I had been unable to do in years. I was still frightened at every fast moving or honking car, and afraid of loud speaking people on the street. But I knew it was time to take that step and move on and move out. I even took the bull from the horns, sort of speak. I applied with the housing authority in the town in which this happened to me since their list was shorter than city's. I was surprised to have been accepted a few months later. So we moved into a spacious three bedroom house which was what we were use to.

My daughter was happier and I was extremely hopeful to a better and brighter future. I got a day job at a major local warehouse and was lucky to have a Monday threw Friday, eight to five schedule. It took me a while to adjust but I never did get close to anyone there. I made a few friends and still kept my personal life extremely private, for how could I function as a normal person amongst so much perfection I thought? But I stuck it out for a few years then one day as I was sitting on my bed my daughter came up to me and asked me if I was happy, because I wasn't fooling her. Truly I was still being haunted by the echoes of my depression and was trying hard to not show it. I didn't want my daughter to know I was still hurting inside, I wanted so bad to keep going, but my daughter knew me too well.

Actually, I was tired of feeling exhausted and drained, without a drop of energy what so ever. It's so difficult to understand the concept of life when you're concentrating on wanting the world to leave you alone. I tried my best to fit in with the rest of the world, but in the end I still hurt.

My Daughter was now having a social life again, working late and hanging out with her friends and co-workers and even though I didn't mind her outings, I just thought that it might have had something to do with me just, moping around and been gloomy all the time, bringing her moral down and it wasn't my intention at all. At least I did appreciate her having patience with me. I don't know what I'd do without her by my side. I even suggested to her that when she married, they could live with me instead of them renting or buying elsewhere.

One day I got the nerve and enrolled in school and become a Truck Driver in a few weeks. I met a girl my age and she had a tremendous amount of confidence I now lacked. So went over the road with the same company and became real good friends.

I quickly realized that no matter where I drove, how far I went to and how pretty it was out their. Everything scared me still. My legs felt weak as I walked into the numerous truck stops. I had tunnel vision eye sight and didn't' want to make eye contact with any body. Unfortunately I only went inside to use the facilities or buy souvenirs when she got off the truck too. But if she didn't get off that neither did I. stayed behind when she didn't get off.

I would not go any where by my self, if she wasn't with me. When she decided to quit that job, I quit too and we both took a greyhound bus home that night. We unfortunately each went our different ways after that interesting and fun adventure. We are still very good friends but now drive for different companies, I drove alone for a few years with a company that was not the greatest in the world, but I gained a lot of experience. Unfortunately I began isolating myself again when I was home, yet kept working nonstop this time. I longed to have a normal life again, so I pushed my self further every time I felt I was falling again.

I cried as hard as I drove, and was terrified when I reached each and every destination knowing it was full of men. Already thinking they could at any given time loose there cool and attach me if they found out I was a female drive and was alone. So I'd stay inside till I was scheduled to deliver my shipment and drove right back light a bat out of hell.

I found I was too sensitive and cried over the memories both good and bad. I was afraid of working again, and having to deal with other people, pervert no doubt. So I try to avoid working long hours. My daughter suggested I get a local driving job, so I'd be closer to her and home every night, but it was easier said then done. But I promised her I'd try and I did, I went out job hunting for a local job.

We lived in a major street so there were a lot of people walking in front of our house night and day. I worried for someone to break in at night. So I'd freeze up when people would stop in front of the house and chat. But I knew I had to be strong for my daughter and I didn't want to loose it again. I wanted my daughter to enjoy a normal life again with me, before she married and decided to move as away.

I kept a journal in which I wrote all of my most intimate secrets and fascinating stories in just before this happened to me. I had it for years and named it "Forever Young" since it was my motto, back then. But I destroyed my Journal right after these jerks destroyed my life. I didn't see any reason to keep recording my life any more since I felt so...Empty.

Chapter 28

My attorney called me in for a formal Deposition and it was once more nerve wrecking as I was asked to repeat the entire occurrences of that night, again. They attached me on a few details that I didn't mention to the Detectives and or Sheriffs when I initially reported the incident. They kept repeatedly asking me even more questions on why I hadn't mentioned certain details the day I made the report.

Their facial expressions changed as I mentioned that it was a total embarrassment to have spoken out in the first place. Besides, it was a time in my life in which I used drugs in a recreational way and was afraid they wouldn't believe me because of my lifestyle and my passed criminal history. Besides I was afraid to speak out because they told me not too.

That day, I felt I had no escape from the officers because I was still in their custody and they were in charge. And they didn't ask for my opinion they just gave me orders on what to do and how to do it. They obviously thought of me as a "not so smart", kind of person, which made me feel stupid to have spoken out. I have been talked down to by people so much that I felt it was a mistake to have come forward. Members of the town as well as the now ex-officers, were at the deposition.

I began doubting my attorney for a while there because I had to face these men again. She slept at night, I didn't! I still thought nobody really cared about me. They just care to look good in a courtroom and impressing the Judge and what goes in their resume.

The state seemed to believe that that therapist cured me by advising me to go out and party. If I could have done that, I wouldn't have had the need for a therapist would I? Well, I didn't think any amount of therapy would cure me any more anyway. So I kept going to the therapist I had found and it was working for me slowly but surely.

These officers had taken my self-esteem away from me, stomped all over my every sexual impulse and taken away my pride. I found it was useless to have gained so much weight on purpose, just so to look unattractive and keep the predators away. My weight problem turned into a permanent thyroid problem. Oh my God! I had just had a tremendous rude awakening.

These men were sitting inside and talking with each other all proud like, as if this was just another day in their usual life. I realized it had nothing to do with the size, shape or figure of a victim that attracts a predator. It's the sick mind and cruel intentions they have to satisfy their own sexual desires. This was a much deeper issue than I thought. This desire came from within them. It was an internal not external problem they had. So I realized these men needed much more therapy than I, and here I've thought I was the one who was broken!

Before this happened, I had taken semi-nude professional pictures of myself because I liked the way I looked and felt so confident with my body. And I felt beautiful and was happy. Because I knew that someday when I was in my golden years I wanted to look back and remember how awesome I looked and felt at age of thirty five, to me of-coarse. I was proud of myself, my body, my mind and my spirit. And even if I didn't have a perfect figure or didn't look as gorgeous as a model to any one else, I did feel good about myself inside and out. And that's all that really mattered to me, and that's why took those pictures.

And now I looked at myself in the mirror and hated to see this big, fat and unhealthy thing I had become so to push perverts away from me. I knew that I had to somehow reverse this unfortunate state of mind. And I would do so one day at a time. Now I felt embarrassed to show my face because I looked terrible.

The day of the deposition I found out that other women had also come forward but wanted to remain anonymous for fear of retaliation. They all mentioned that they too were treated the same way I did by these officers. I found out through the investigating process that the Police Department was aware of these and other problems yet ignored their accusations. I know now that if I had gone to the townsmen or the police like another girl did, they would have ignored me as well. Unfortunately, the other girls didn't come forward. I can't say I blame them, but I wish they knew they weren't alone. And that together we can make a difference. I also found out that night I was not only falsely arrested but also that the officers had cancelled the tow truck they told me they requested the day they pulled me over. They told me I was being arrested for warrants and being drunk. But they lied to me, I heard them brewing up a scheme after realizing I wasn't drunk and passed the sobriety tests they conducted on me. And most importantly, I did not have any warrants as they claimed. I also felt that these officer's faults went unnoticed therefore went undocumented and ignored by their police department as well as our justice system.

Chapter 29

After this gathering for the deposition, my house was mysteriously shot at, two nights in a row. The first night, they shot at the living room window which led to the street. My uncle was visiting us from out of town and was going to spend a few days with us. He was getting ready to go to asleep on the couch underneath that window. I was standing in front of my uncle providing him with a blanket and was in clear view of the window. That's when we heard the shots and the curtain moved. My daughter called the police and they took there time getting their. When they finally arrived they said it was no big deal, they weren't real bullets they were BB's from a BB gun they said.

But by the next night, we had just returned from dropping off my uncle at my mother's house. We were getting ready for bed as my daughter planned on sleeping in my room with me for fear of them shooting again. We were once again targeted while I was standing in front of my bedroom window. This time I ran outside immediately after the shooting ignoring my daughter's plea for me not to go outside. But I saw no one. This too, according to town police, was ruled as a random shooting.

And even though my house was the only residence that was shot at, they refused to further investigate the incident. But they were only suspicions not accusations. Not in a town full of officers whom are experts at shooting their targets, both on and off duty. I confronted them with my speculations and they just blew me off saying it was just that, speculations. That was not random, not twice, not to me, I had no enemies. I couldn't make any accusations because I didn't see anyone and don't know who shot at me.

They never did it again and they did not even take the time to investigate, and worst of all I had to pay to replace the windows. The Police Department stated it was a freak coincidence and not a direct target towards me. A few days later I noticed constant police cars parked a few feet from my house, and that intimidated me very much. They'd drive off as soon as I walked towards them. Of coarse I didn't want to be calling my attorney every day but today I know I should have, but its in the past now, all I could do now, was move forward.

The Officers would stare me down every time I'd run into them, which was yet another coincidence. I started to run into the many police officers and the chief of police constantly. And frankly I did not want to stay in that town any longer. They tried to intimidate me with there fierce looks and I must say, it worked. I gave up and left anyway, we moved out of that house and I never reveal my physical address anymore. For fear of someone coming back to shoot at us again and making seem like it was random, again. I have realized, or felt that most people are not too supportive of victims. Either because it makes them uncomfortable or they just don't want to be there for you. Or they've just never been through a similar situation. The ones that are supportive are the once that have unfortunately, either been violated in any way, shape or form.

I experienced several night mares which horrified me so much I dreaded night fall. In one horrible nightmare I'm the cook at a restaurant. While cooking, I'm standing in front of a huge Chinese Wok full of boiling oil. All of a sudden my right arm is involuntarily being pushed very slowly into the Wok, and for some strange reason all I do is cry and watch in horror. I feel paralyzed and helpless as I watch my arm slip away and become nothing but bone. I'm in extreme pain and I can't do anything physically to pull away. When I finally look back to see the person who disintegrated my arm I realize it was one of the Officers. I then start crying and screaming and unable to pull away. I then wake up screaming and holding my arm and I swear I could still physically feel the pain.

In another dream my ex boyfriend and I drove home and parked outside our apartment. My boyfriend was unlocking the front door and they shoot an arrow straight through his throat. As I get out of the car and run to his side, an officer twists my arm back so much that he pops it out of place and it just hangs their as they beat me till I can't move. But I am conscience the entire time feeling the excruciating pain.

And again, I wake up and can't move or feel my arm, at first I thought I was sleeping on top of my arm, but my daughter slept in the same room with me a few times to watch me, the poor dear. And it wasn't so. Unfortunately, my dreams had become a huge problem to me so I'd stay up at night in fear of having these or other terrible nightmares.

In one nightmare I'm looking in horror and unable to scream while one of the Officers is forcing my arm in a meat grinder. I'm squirming with the unbearable pain. I look up and see people walking in front of me but nobody seems to care, much less help me. People walk pass me as if it is the most normal thing in the world and move on. But when the grinder reaches my shoulder, my pain worsens and I wake up screaming again.

My daughter suggested I try to take charge and figure out a way to change what I didn't like about my dreams. She said the counselor she had as a child taught her how to conquer her nightmares and rule her dreams. She shared this information with me but nothing seemed to work for me. I use to comfort her at night when she was a child and now it was the other way around. Well I kept tying by following her the advice and I still have nightmares some times but their not as bad any more. I've read books of victims of similar crimes and unfortunately, more than half said the same crime happened to then twice or more times by totally different people in there lives. They all claim to run that horrible bad luck or be magnets to men that try to take advantage of them. I think that is amazingly disappointing and frightening.

Chapter 30

One day as I gave some advice to a friend who was grieving her Brother's death. I read the letter before sending it and realized I could use my own advice. Someone had shared this with me a long time ago and it worked for me in the past.

I said "my condolences to you my friend. I found out sometime ago, that when you throw yourself to working harder or help other people with their problems. You tend to focus on them and forget your own problems. When you reach your home keep busy until you go to sleep and pray for even more work the next day. I found, that God carries your load for you until you are strong enough to handle it on your own again. God knows what we can handle and help us with the rest so we're obviously doing ok. Which is why we give him Thanks and Praise all of the time, not just when we are sad, gloomy and alone? It's worked for me in the past and that's how I know it will work for you too."

And then I realized that I could use the same advice. I remembered that this was the way for me to recuperate. But of coarse why hadn't I thought of this before?

My life was happening all around me and I was missing out, I was not a part of it. Like sitting in a corner listening to everyone, but can't give your opinion. My bills were piling up because I felt uncomfortable leaving my house. I relived the past whenever I left my home, so this made it impossible for me to even enjoy my new house. I was like a real, living and breathing invisible ghost.

I prayed to not get pulled over again because, I didn't think I could handle that and I didn't want to worry about it anymore. Unfortunately, I knew that if I called the Help Crisis Hotline they'd advice me to go for an evaluation and possible inpatient services. And I refused to be institutionalized for something these jerks did to me. They have already taken so much from me and I will not be locked down as If it were my fault. They're the once whom should be put away.

I gave an old friend some advice of how she should move on and not look back. And it kills me to think I was unable to do that, myself! Why am I still here? Why can't I just get over this and move on or just curl up and die already? I felt horribly trapped in my own house, unable to go outside, time kept passing me by and I had had enough. It is very depressing to know that some people never really do recover from traumatic experiences. They go through life dragging their feet and I was not going to be a prisoner in my own skin any longer.

Chapter 31

I wasn't living I was just existing. Existing is just breathing and a waste of good oxygen that others were happy to take advantage of, and that was not enough. The mind is an extremely powerful muscle and it does overpower the soul, your soul will take over all of your emotions good or bad if you allow it. Unfortunately, my soul was as low as my self esteem. I was just a lump on the couch, taking up energy and space. So I began to evaluate my situation in a different manner then create a strategy and made guidelines to follow.

I knew that the horrific trauma I had suffered was not my fault. I needed to know and understand that I had to stop feeling guilty for what someone else did to. And that I had no control of the extent these people had hurt me.

I definitely needed to stop fighting and continue getting professional help until I really felt I could handle my own life again.

I needed to get a job in which was suitable for me and allowed me to be happy and proud of what I did.

I had always worked out my problems and supported my family on my own, and I wanted to begin today. I was done crying and feeling sorry for myself, I had reached my level of pity and start working on my list as well as work, worship and help others.

Someone needs to follow up on severely depressed people because we are not ok. We are sinking deeper and deeper by the minute and nobody is even realizing it until we become another statistic. It is not fair to our families, our country or us. I confronted a therapist with my opinion on one of my visits, and the next day she gave me a call. Wow, I thought, she only called me because I complained. You know that wasn't necessary any more, because I had made a decision to go out the next day and get a job and take back what these two jerks took away from me. My nerve, my happiness and my self! The center had been great to me but now it was time to move on. I found that many people, mostly men, are turned on sexually, when you describe in details about other sexual encounters you've had, including Rape. That is repulsive to me. I was going to take back dignity and pride these men took away from me. I didn't feel I had much help or guidance so I wanted to share with you what I had gone through. It was time for me to go out and face the world again. I want to educate myself so they can convict offenders that think of themselves as more powerful than others. Didn't they know not to use and abuse women? Don't they understand they 'v completely destroyed my life? Wasn't there Mother good to them? Wasn't their father ever around? What? What was their excuse for their stupid behavior towards me? And why didn't the City, when they hired these men, investigate their passed a little more and take in consideration that their passed wasn't that good? Why didn't they question there flaws?

Personally I have completed many questionnaires to "determine if I'm eligible" for the job and be honest enough for them or not. They also supervise employees on a constant basis, and have surprise visits to check their employees. This is even done at local convenient stores and restaurants all over the United States and the World. So I don't understand why this Town couldn't do that with their officers, after all, they are, ONLY the Police Officers.

I was just so tired of asking questions and not getting any answers. I had to stop! I had to let God determine their fate as he has with mine. I was tired of fighting a past that I'd never be able to change. And I found myself praying the Lords prayer on a daily basis as well as a simple prayer that kept me sane and made so much sense to me for so long.

The Serenity prayer I was taught at a twelve step program.

"God grant me the serenity to change the things I can, The Courage to change the things I can't and the Wisdom to know the difference".

I was blessed with a great job and was learning to socialize again. Little by little I started going out and attempted to have fun with as many people as I could. I push myself a little further every day, and I have come across so many more perverts along the way. I still struggle today as I handle each situation differently as they come, without having an anxiety attack. I have found ways to cope with my depression by knowing that it's not up to me, to punish, convict and live in a prison like life for other's mistake. I am a happier person now as I smile, laugh and live all over again. I still cry, kick and scream at times when I find myself struggling to solve a problem I can't handle and find my self all by myself. It's awful to not trust men any more but I'm still working on it. I know now that I can throw a fit on the floor then get up, dust myself off and keep going.

I had a conversation with a barmaid where I met up with some friends after work one day. And she said she had quit a former job at a construction company due to men sexually harassing her and every girl at that work place. Her former boss scolded these men for doing this to her but mentioned that her boss was worse then the employees. Wow! And all she did was quit her job, and now she's working at a bar. She said that the men are somehow more respectful their and they have stricter rules when it came to men disrespecting women. Isn't that ironic? But it is good for her and her self esteem.

I would like to some day achieve what I think the system has neglected to do. To give offenders a harsher punishment and be registered as sexual offenders. Because this is what they are Sex Offenders, I think they deserve to serve a jail time sentence just like the rest of the sexual offenders. I'm not too educated in laws and regulations yet, so I wouldn't even know were to begin. But just like every other civilian I'd like to feel protected by our local law enforcement officers. Sometimes I wonder how many more women they have taken advantage of in many other ways but still feel unable come forward or even talk about it.

Women are unable to confide in anyone for the fear of having others treat them as if it was their fault. There are agencies that offer free services and counseling for victims like me. No matter whom I talk to, or what I read and how much forget about it, I still lived in a nightmare I couldn't wake up from. There has got to be a way for me to educate myself about the laws and regulations in which to help make a difference to assist others whom have not come forward yet. There has to be more to our country than this. There has to be more that we can do to help the victim than to say, "move on, get over it, your strong, you will survive."

Chapter 32

I landed a great job which was a challenging and demanding tough job. And I have always pushed myself to the limits so it was really rewarding to me as well as exhausting. But I had to keep going for my sake. Besides, if I would have stayed at home laying on the couch, crying all the time, then these offenders would have won again.

In the summer of 2006 I got a job driving a water truck and a dump truck and I actually enjoyed my job. A few months later I was placed on a fuel/service truck in which I was terrified of. I was so afraid of hauling fuel since I had never worked with any kind of fuel before. I mean the truck had two kinds of hydraulic fluids, gasoline, three kinds of oils, an air compressor and a pressure washer. It also had so many tools I was unfamiliar with. But I learned as I went and adjusted to my new job. Every day I was thrilled to have gotten that opportunity to learn something new every single day. I felt so privileged since it gave me a chance to learn to operate most of the construction heavy equipment as well as work on them. I had to move the equipment around and being mechanically inclined was part of the job. So I learned new skills on a daily basis because there was something new and totally different every single day, so my job became my hobby. I learned to distinguish the types of equipment and what kind of fluids they carried as well as the capacity they each held.

Those first few months working on the fuel truck were the scariest for me since I was still learning and adjusting to different situations. I also took Hazmat courses and became osha certified which is a big deal in this business. They constantly switched my partners for the first few months because they all seemed to complain about different things including the long hours we had to work.

Thankfully they finally gave me a great partner whom was a man with a lot of experience, very talented and extremely patient with me. He taught me even more essential work ethics I never knew existed and or mattered. He showed me how to take the tire pressure and that they are all different. Change the cutting edges on the various front end loaders and bull dozers and the rippers. We then created a great routine that was both rapidly and efficient. We blew air filters, fueled and grease all the machines in a timely manner and maintained the company pick ups too. I even learned how to install a bulk fuel tank in back of a pick up, wire it up and bolt it down every thing. That year I joined the local union and I felt privileged to have my picture on two of their quarterly magazines, once in fall of 2008 and the other in spring 2010.

I was extremely proud that my picture was actually chosen to be placed in our union magazine. I was thrilled and it boosted my esteem up as woman which was an accomplishment I thought I'd never reach. I felt so appreciated and that gave me the energy to work harder and give it my all. I woke up every morning with a huge smile and anxious to start the day. My partner and I became a great team, and I became his understudy since he knew how to run and fix all the machines we had. We averaged seventy hours a week for over four years. Sometimes we had to work over eighty hours a week and, even thought we were exhausted, we never complained.

We both had our good days and we had our bad. And some times disagreed with each but we always stay until we accomplished our demanding daily work. I was thrilled to have gotten a partner that was as eager, hard working and dedicated as I was. We became accustomed to so many hours that when the time came for us to only work sixty hours a week, we didn't know what to do with so much time. The time came in which we were separated because the company bought another fuel truck and we each had our own truck now. But we still stayed close and worked in conjunction so the work load wouldn't lean on just one of us. We were an inseparable team and took our job very seriously. We rapidly created a new technique to service all of our machines. It was a truly amazing experience for me.

I had educated myself in the construction business as far as being able to carry the work load by myself now. When my partner took vacation or was unable to work, I was now trusted to do the work alone, with out a partner. I had a tremendous amount of confidence in knowing that the company now acknowledged me to be most capable to complete the two man job by my self.

I even trained other men that came aboard who requested too want to join our fuel family and that was a great accomplishment for me. Unfortunately only one man made our team. Before I knew it, the years had gone by and my past was nearly inexistent, I was still careful to not trust any man and was afraid of having a serious relationship. But I had become a little more socially active now.

Wow, I thought I'd never feel this good in my entire life again, but I did, and I was on the road to recovery. This job had given me that chance to look towards a brighter future I needed. It inspired me to believe in myself and loose that fear for every single man I came in contact with.

I even came to forget that more than ninety five percent of the company employees were all men. I loved that they all respected me as an individual and was treated as an equal. Occasionally there were men that tried to look down on me for been a woman. Or some would treat me cruel but I learned to deal with it and they learned to accept me as a coworker and that was another great accomplishment for me. I had spent years in isolation as if I was a prisoner and subconsciously dragged myself as dead weight. I now felt free and so relieved. I slowly began to regain that confidence again and gotten control of my life. Still today when my past wants to creep up and cruelly haunt me, I find ways to deal with it, because I am worth it. I am worth having a normal life again, better then the one I had before all this happened to me.

I still lack the confidence to trust and date men but I pray that too will happen soon for me. I pray others have the courage I lacked to speak out the night these fools took advantage of me. I hope the Police Department become more responsible and have learned a lesson or two on self-discipline, self control and respect for others. Some of us would still like to think of them as trustworthy in case we find ourselves in trouble. Unfortunately because of these perverted, some of us can never think of Policemen as truly honest. I hope they do have more Supervision, surprise visits and inspections, just like the rest of the world. Especially in the rural areas where there are most likely not enough Officers.

This is why they feel they have more freedom, and get away with whatever they want. Sad to say, some officers are in need of major supervision. But we can only hope our local police department would hire trusted, mature and loyal men. I had to changed my lifestyle and not trust anyone completely, and I know it isn't healthy but that is an unfortunate side effect I was left with. My method of therapy was to become a workaholic, living in constant communication with my family and having a spiritual life.

Writing has kept my sanity and been my most helpful form of therapy. And I decided that I was not going to allow my tragedy to last a life time. I turned my life around and stopped counting the times I fell into my sweet ole comfortable depression, and feeling like a failure.

I picture these Officers out with their wives and kids living there life as if nothing ever happened to them. Because they'll never understand that it happened to me. They don't deserve for me to spend the rest of my life a lonely, angry bitter person while they are leading happy lives. I will continue to be a wonderful productive member of society. I will not have remorse, guilt or shame because I was the victim, and I strongly believe that I did not deserve the tragedy I suffered.

Chapter 33

I learned that most rape victims blame themselves and are afraid others will blame them too, and that is why they don't want to come forward. But even thought it was extremely difficult for me and my daughter to go through this, because you do. I would definitely advice victims to come forward if they have been raped, molested or violated in any way shape or form.

Most prisoners when they are attacked, violated or raped by police officers or guards, keep it to them selves. They are treated like they don't deserve to be heard or respected, like they don't have a voice. Some people think prisoners deserve to be mistreated, stepped on or humiliated. People tend to convict us before and after the judge and or jury does, and that is not fair. We have feelings too, and we may have made mistakes but that is no reason for others to make us feel as worthless as they are. They have no right to ridicule prisoners because of there past. Unfortunately, some of us begin to believe that we are nothing but an instrument for higher author figures. We can not allow them to win. We are able to pick ourselves up and show them we are higher class than they are. We are worth saving, we disserve to stick together and to be heard. The only way a predator will understand that he is the one who needs help is if we report them and give them harsher punishments.

They need a life time of therapy because it is a mental illness that becomes physical. A parole officer I spoke to some time ago confirmed a theory I heard. He said that a sexual offender will strike over and over again because that's whom he is, not some thing he did.

I looked up these definitions in the dictionary and this is what I found.

Sexual: Of relating to, Involving, or characteristics of sex, or the sex organs and their functions.

Predator: An organism that lives by preying on other organisms

One that victimizes, Plunders, or Destroys, Especially for ones own gain.

Offender: (the verb offend)

To violate or transgress, (a criminal, religious, or moral law)

It can cause resentful displeasure, irritate, annoy or anger.

Rape: An act of plunder, violent seizure, or Abuse

I still live alone, for I have trouble finding some one I can trust. It is important for me to share with you a little bit about what happened to me because it took an amazing amount of courage for me to finally speak out. But If I wouldn't have had my daughter's support and love by my side, I never would have come forward.

I have learned that no matter where I go and how I look, there will always be Sexual Offenders in disguises and given the chance, they will make their move. They are people like you and me, walking amongst us everyday, which is why we have to always be aware of our surroundings never take anybody for granted.

I've completely stopped my late night shopping I use to do before and never even thought twice about. I ask to be escorted by a trusted group of friends if I don't feel safe. And I would definitely never get out of my car if I would get pulled over after dark. I know now that I can call 911 and verify that Police have called in and verified my information and I can stay on the line with them until I am dismissed by the 911 Operator not the Officer. You could contact your local Sheriff's Office for Local telephone numbers. I wouldn't want any one to go through the disgrace and humiliation that I was put threw.

The last time I saw these two Officers, was in court. At the court sentencing we were advised to walk up to the last flight of stairs at the court house which lead to a rear door of the courtroom and leads directly to the Judge's office. This is done to protect the victim's identity as well as to prepare you before you are faced with your attacker. I think this essential and necessary since the last thing you want is to ride the same elevator or be seated next to your attacker in the hallway.

When the Judge, the attorneys, the media and the court reporter were all ready to begin, we were escorted into the court room. I was nervous and scared but anxious to start the final stage of the most awful nightmare of my life. My daughter was as nervous as I was, but she didn't show it as much as I did. She stood straight and firm, looking right into there direction. As if she could slap them with her eyes. I looked at her and wished I could be as strong as her. We looked at each other and smiled and held hands the entire time and I knew we were going to be ok. I was surprised to see a few inmates sitting there waiting to be trial too I guess.

The inmates too were mad dogging the men that had violated me.

I have to say this gave me a sort of comfort as they too I felt were angry at these men.

I have to admit I was hurting inside to have not seen any of my family members there, by my side. I wished they would all come running threw the door making excuses for being late. But I didn't want to worry about anybody else just then, I didn't want to be distracted. I wanted to focus on my Lamaze like breathing that was beginning to feel like an anxiety attack coming on. Tears quickly built up and came out one by one and rolled down my face. My daughter then squeezed my hand and I shut my eyes a few seconds, saying a prayer and then was called up by the Judge. He then apologized for what these men did to me, since he knew neither one of them had apologized then read their sentence out load.

What?! A slap on the wrist felt like, "just don't do it again". I thought to myself.

They each received five years probation, four hundred hours community service and attend several sex offenders' classes! So my unanswered question was and still is, if they were ordered to attend sex offender's classes, why weren't they ordered to register as sex offenders? I felt that this was a huge miscarriage of justice. Why didn't they get jail time like I did for not paying my tickets? What made their offence less grave than mine?

But no matter what I thought or how I felt, that was there sentence. And once more, I didn't have a say so. The assistant district attorneys kept telling me it was ok and was going to be fine. And all I could think about was they just didn't want me to loose it and tell them off in the court room. I could have gotten arrested for lashing out at them, but they can walk away with the satisfaction of not going to jail. That's life I suppose.

Chapter 34

At the officer's sentencing I was able to read my victim impact statement. To the bossier one whom turned out to have been the sergeant and said he couldn't remember which one of all the girls he had done this too, I was. And to the officer that said, "It was only oral sex he didn't do anything sexually to me, besides, he was only following orders"!

I said:

"I don't think you'll ever know how what you and your partner did to me that night has affected and changed my life as well as my family's for ever. I don't think I will ever completely recover from the humiliation and embarrassment you have put me through. You both chose to take advantage of your badge and your authority as police officers, and you didn't care if I had a mother or a daughter who cared about me. You arrested me, I was your prisoner and not as educated as you. But because of your education, your uniform and your authority you were able to outsmart me and lie to me by telling me I had warrants, when in fact I did not. All you wanted was to satisfy your own sexual needs but you have ruined mine to this day. I have not being able to trust any body thanks to your disgusting ideas. When you became officers you took an oath and were entrusted to help, protect and serve the community from perverts like yourselves. Not help yourself to lonely women that appeared vulnerable, as I was at the time. But all you thought of was to gratify your very small ego of a man. And you claimed to follow orders. Orders! From a superior whom happens to be even more pathetic than you. For an educated police officer you sure are a stupid excuse of a man without a conscience or common sense to think of his own. My cat has more common sense than you do. You are men who will never be able to become leaders in life because you are unable to think for yourselves, and I thought I was bad. A person who can't think for them self are worthless and useless in this world. So I think you're in for a bumpy ride in this life. But I am extremely grateful to our legal system for them stripping you from your badge, guns and uniform because you are a disgrace to our society as a police officers. You are cowards and men without values, morals nor integrity. Sitting outside of a bar in hopes of taking advantage of a drunken woman is considered a predator stalking its prey. And that is was you did to me, only I wasn't drunk and contrary to what you said to me, they did listen to me. Because not every one is as sick as you are. There are professional people that actually do there job correctly. But I realize today that God must have been watching over me that night just like he made sure you didn't go to prison for this. At least I know that as of today, I can go home knowing that there are two less perverted officers off the streets. No amount of counseling has been able to help me overcome the humiliation you both have put me through. But today I am thankful that this issue is resolved and I can somehow put this behind me and never see you again. I pray for God to someday teach me the art of forgiveness so I can forgive you, because I need that for my spiritual growth."

One of the men's lawyers interrupted me when I was reading my victims impact statement in court and in front of many people including the local media, his family and my daughter. This attorney was given a fine for doing this. So I was told, but I have my doubts of course.

Chapter 35

None of my family members showed up at neither of my courts. I would have loved to see everyone there because I needed all the support in the world that day. I felt the weight of the world on my shoulders and my world was crumbling down. My daughter sat by my side and held my hand real tight through out the entire time, and so did the assistant district attorney on my other side. They were with me through out the entire court procedure and that made me feel a sense of security and as if I had the entire world at my side.

When the court was over and we were dismissed and walked out through the rear door again because they do respect the victim's identity and privacy. The now ex-officers were attacked by the crowd of media. The bossier one, who was the sergeant, had no one by his side and after he was dismissed, he stormed out of there avoiding everyone and disappeared through the crowd of media.

The other one practically ran out into the hallway, ignoring the media whom wanted to get his statement on camera as well, but they ran as fast as they could out of their and I believe one hid in the men's room. We waited in the judges chambers till the media left and we stopped crying a bit. Then we were accompanied out of the building. As we reached the elevator, one of the local and most popular news reporters was waiting for us. She asked if she could interview me or my daughter without showing our face or giving out names.

My daughter thought it'd be a good idea and take that next step in recovery, and so did I. We sat in the hallway ready for the interview, but before we began, I looked over her shoulder and told her that my offender was behind her. But when they turned the camera towards him he ran again, leaving his female companion to catch up to him. I ended up going through with the interview and that was the beginning of my recovery healing process. That reporter made me realize that day that I was not the only one that had been violated and was going through this nightmare.

Off camera, the reporter told me that in her career, she had interviewed many others victims before. And they shared with her their experience, strength and hope, and the recovery process was painful, but a definite triumph. She also said she was very proud of my courage and I should be proud of myself as well. She made me realized that I held the key to my own healing process that would lead to my total recovery. And I refused to feel like a completely defeated victim for the rest of my life. I was a survivor not just another statistic. As long as I believed in myself, these cowards were not going take away any more from me then they already had. I wasn't going to live in the dark any more because of their stupidity. I was going to fight back by taking the reigns of my life again and starting over, but I would recover because I still believe in god.

The court reporter also came out to find me and shook my hand. She congratulated me for my statement as she felt it had made an impact in the way she would view others from now on.

She also said she thought I had left quit an impression on everyone that had heard me in their. Other people whom were in the courtroom, whom I never found out who they were, came out to give me a hug and shake my hand as well and apologize for what I had been through. And others couldn't believe these people had stooped that low and thought they would continue to get away with it. These men had lost more than I realized up to that point. Their career must have made them feel very important and they ruined that the day I spoke out. The world would now be aware of their embarrassing little secret that was exposed when they decided to humiliate me. And it was going to be good challenge for them to have to explain their past to their new employer. Neither one of these men showed any remorse at all. I choose to believe that the only thing they are sorry about is for my speaking out. And I am very sorry to still feel they left me completely broken.

On our drive home that day, I felt a weight had lifted off of my shoulders and I looked over to my daughter whom had been so calm and cool throughout the entire proceeding. Said she had gotten the feeling the officers looked worried they might receive a jail sentencing or harsher punishment.

I asked her why and she said she noticed that one of them was constantly nagging about something to his lawyer which I didn't notice. I didn't dare look into their fears piercing eyes for a hint of fear still lingered inside me. I was fighting my intense feeling to lash out at them and cause them great bodily harm. But come on whom was I trying to kid, I would never be able to hurt anyone as they hurt me.

Offenders are people from all kinds of background levels of education and lack of education. We as human beings should valor ourselves and do everything possible so others respect us even better than we respect ourselves. Never loose our dignity or allow others to violate our sense of self respect and self esteem. We must always focus on our inter beauty because we are worth all that we crave in this world. We are as beautiful as we want to be, but have to watch out for wolves that may change us in a heart beat. Violators come in many ways, shape and disguised. But you should never allow anyone to ridicule you in anyway shape or form or trick you into doing anything humiliating and embarrassing for the joy of others. These people are sexual offenders! Make no mistake about that, we the surviving victims are living proof of that! Some victims do recover, some never have a chance, some are never given that chance and some never learn how! But I do believe that with God all is possible, I prayed for a miracle and he answered my prayers! Unfortunately, I had made the decision to block him out and feel the pain instead, and that was a huge mistake.

Chapter 36

Every 2 minutes, someone in America is sexually assaulted. 683,000 people are raped each year. Sadly only 2% of rapists are imprisoned or convicted. Sexual assault is probably the most hostile crimes out there. It is one of the most violent crimes aside from murder. Yet these two crimes go hand in hand some times. In this day in age, society looks away from this crime and are filled with disbelief and doubt. This might be the reason only about 40% of assaults are actually reported to the police.

Only 6% of rapists will ever spend a day in jail; so why you ask should anyone report this crime if there is little or any outcome? Because of the lack of response for us victims and these numbers alone are too many reasons. Even task forces and committees on violence against women quickly tend to limit their discussions to domestic violence. When rape presents itself in about 1/3 of domestic violence cases, no other crime calls out for justice more than rape. This has to change. Many women and men are ashamed when this happens to them, even though they shouldn't be. Most of us think of rape as only happening to kids, but these numbers are surprisingly true.

- 22% of rapes happen under 12 yrs of age
- 32% are between 12 – 17 yrs old
- 29% are between 18 – 24 yrs old
- 17% are over 25 yrs old

This information is from the (USCU Rape Prevention

Education website) but these statistics change on a daily basis.

Rape and or any kind of sexual assault crimes not only harm and violate the physical form of the victim. It also consumes your mind, your body and soul. It degrades your human rights in the most intimate way. I was sexually assaulted more than 9yrs ago by two police officers. They arrested me, took advantage of me then released me. These men were charged then convicted about 2yrs later for violation of a woman in custody. They were in jail less than 4 hours, only as long as the booking process took place. They were only given 5yrs probation when I am suffering a life time sentence of this shame and fear they put me through. Even though you must move on and most victims do, we will always have this scare like tattoo in our souls that will carry till our resting day. 6 months following a rape 50% of victims lose their jobs and 50% have suffered the break-up of a relationship. The law doesn't understand this pain. Unfortunately rape is the most costly of all crimes to our society.

I encouraged victims to focus on educating and assisting others with our criminal justice system. Most women are reluctant to report rape and sexual assault for fear of law enforcement not doing enough for the victim. This, to an extent is an unfortunate truth.

Law enforcement in many cases mistreat the victim, in fact they attack them. Unfortunately, many people think rape is a very easy accusation to make but very difficult to prove. Some times it's a sort of "he said she said" problem. Some times rape lack the physical evidence but has many advantages to solve a case that other crimes lack.

The victim usually knows who the perpetrator is, or has details that are critical to the investigation. Unfortunately, not many officers know how, or want to deal with these kinds of cases since it requires talking and dealing with the victims personally. And it is as uncomfortable for them as it is for the victim. When you report a crime your privacy is invaded as well as your entire life. You feel humiliated and uncomfortable as the day you were violated.

Very few rape cases are prosecuted, because no victim is easier to make go away then a rape victim. The victims are usually forced to undergo hours of interviewing and interrogation by officials who mistreat them or treat them like it's their fault, so the victims understandably retreat. This usually leads officers into saying the victim was uncooperative and bailed, so it must not be true. Victims do not get the justice and protection that is their constitutional right. Many victims like me, do not receive the support, guidance or education to the many assistance available to victims. I had my daughter, but there was only so much she could help me with. I was unfortunately unaware of all the assistance and advocate programs available to victims.

Many victims won't receive a proper justice response without the skillful assistance of a skillful advocate when she requires it. During our investigation we found out that this small town's police department had many other unreported flaws. They had had reported incidents like mine before, but were never pursued or were just ignored. Thankfully these victim's statements helped my case to be stronger, since they had been through very similar situations as well. Unfortunately these women were afraid to come forward. No one can make the decision for you or force you to come forward and speak out. But for our sake I hope you do.

I learned that these officers also had several other reports against them aside from the women they had violated. Even though I believe my case could have been much stronger, I had enough evidence as well as their confession to help my case. This gave me the confidence to pursue my case until they were convicted.

75% of victims experience some kind of guilt, making it that much harder to report. Every state has different rape laws and statue of limitations in which to report and prosecute sexual assault cased.

Most rape victims don't report the attack to the police immediately. It's very common for victims to wait a few days, months or even years before telling anyone. When they finally do tell someone, it's usually a friend, or a counselor but not the police. In my case, my attackers were police men, which made it even more difficult to confide in their own.

It's taken me over 9yrs to talk about this. And it's still difficult for me to suppress such sad emotions which automatically arise without warning. I know there are many women out there that have been raped and keeping it all bottled up inside.

In fact 1 in 6 women will be assaulted in their lifetime.

Just imagine, if not you, then your daughter, sister, mother, aunt, friend or even grandma, have or will be assaulted this year. That is a scary thought as I fit all of the above.

Chapter 37

I am a mother, a daughter, a sister, an aunt, a friend, and now a grandmother. Even though some attackers are given a slap on the hand when they are convicted; they are labeled as "sex offenders". Most offenders will have to register for the rest of their lives. They were ordered to get sexual offenders counseling, but the court of law did not consider them sexual offenders.

Rape is different for many. The law requires a different outcome for every case. I felt that because I was not a child, they determined I didn't hurt as much. Would they have given them only 5yrs probation if I was a child, or a teenager? So what if they would have killed me, would that have been enough to consider it as Rape?

I'll remember their names and faces for ever and are imbedded in my mind. Their voices will forever haunt me. With out the items I kept with their DNA and their full confession, perhaps we would have had a difficult time convicting them. Always keep what ever evidence you can from your attackers, for you never know what can help bring them to justice.

It's important to get as much as you can from them. There spit, blood, hair, even scratching them can get physical evidence. Save your clothes, don't throw them away. I know how disgusting you feel afterwards but don't shower. Go to the hospital, they will help.

Don't be afraid. I know you may feel alone but you're not. I can promise you that. I can only hope all victims have support from their family, but some, like me, will not. I had my family's support after I came home and they watched the news. But do not allow this to discourage you. Don't allow your criminal past be an obstacle for you to get help. Don't allow any kind of law enforcement agents to violate you and get away with it. Reach out to friends, to the rape victims hotline, or to people you trust. Someone will help you get through it.

I found peace through my daughter whom I gave birth to, and through my grate job. I refuse to stay a victim for the rest of my life. And now we know there are people who care even though they don't know me. The RAINN program is the nation's largest anti-sexual assault organization. There website www.rainn.org has all the information you need, from what numbers to call, to where you can go and even have survivor stories.

You will also find the millions of actresses and famous people that have suffered the same injustice we have. This website is a blessing to people like us. There are many others, don't just let this go. We don't deserve to be hurt and put aside. Don't forget that.

As a victim, I do know how it feels and what we go through. But as a survivor I am mad. Mad at the fact that the government and our society turns there shoulder to this crime. More needs to be done. Rapists are walking among our children, our family, and us! Sadly these statistics show that 50% of rapists, will rape again. The criminal justice system has knowledge of these statistics yet accept it and aid offenders anyway. Sometimes I look back and shed a tear but it's mostly for the liberated feeling I have that I released my broken past.

Sincerely you're Friend

L.L

www.ingramcontent.com/pod-product-compliance
Lightning Source LLC
Chambersburg PA
CBHW051431280526
45785CB00003B/1248